Thank you for the opportunity to review *Keys to the Kingdom*. Your book is a powerful, motivating guide for all people who want to strengthen their relationships with Jesus Christ. Your writing is clear, and your faith and determination are clearly demonstrated on every page.
- Publications Editor

Great insight about grouping the parables into categories: Salvation, Prayer, Forgiveness, etc. This will make it easier to connect the parable to life's situations when needed. I can't wait to buy copies for my class.
- Sunday School Women's Bible Teacher
Breeding, Kentucky

Well formatted, and easy to understand the subject and material.
- Youth Minister, North River Church,
Tuscaloosa, Alabama

No study of the life and teachings of Jesus Christ is complete without an understanding of the parables He taught. Most books that cover parables generally cover the better-known ones. They avoid the difficult, challenging, and obscure.

Art Zacher and Doug Peterson break that tradition in this book, covering dozens of the parables spoken by Jesus. When Jesus shared these parables with individuals and groups, He challenged them to live a godly life – and that challenge is still relevant today.

Each parable is set in its historic setting, with previous and following events noted. The authors reveal where Jesus spoke each parable, who His audience was, and what each one means. Each parable is classified with other parables on the same topic for easy reference.

Get detailed insights on what Jewish people were thinking as they waited for their Messiah along with insights on the practical applications of Jesus' teachings today with the lessons in *Keys to the Kingdom.*

- Fundamental Baptist minister

Keys to the Kingdom
PARABLES OF JESUS

by Art Zacher
and
Doug Peterson

WESTBOW
PRESS®
A DIVISION OF THOMAS NELSON
& ZONDERVAN

WestBow Press books may be ordered through booksellers or by contacting:

WestBow Press
A Division of Thomas Nelson & Zondervan
1663 Liberty Drive
Bloomington, IN 47403
www.westbowpress.com
844-714-3454

Scripture taken from the King James Version of the Bible.

ISBN: 978-1-6642-4896-0 (sc)
ISBN: 978-1-6642-4897-7 (hc)
ISBN: 978-1-6642-4895-3 (e)

Library of Congress Control Number: 2021922303

Print information available on the last page.

WestBow Press rev. date: 1/27/2022

ACKNOWLEDGEMENTS

This book has been a long overdue and prolonged study for many years. The parables of Jesus are some of the most quoted portions of the Holy Scriptures. Researched, assembled, "shaken and stirred", reviewed, and then studied some more, then tested by teaching and preaching, this has been a wonderful labor of love of the Gospels for many years, first independently, then together by both of us.

We both would like to acknowledge and thank our faithful wives, who encouraged us in our labors to complete this work, with tireless editing, typing, then reviewing our many drafts (original and corrected). None of this could have occurred without their wonderful, patient encouragement, and faithful partnership and the help of our loving wives. Thank you, ladies.

Many people write journals, diaries, and notebooks, often with dreamed intents of getting them formally printed and turned into books to be shared. The only way that usually occurs is with the professional help of publishers. We definitely want to thank all the folks at WestBow Press for their patience and professionalism in helping us to accomplish this task, and see this book come to fruition. We couldn't have done it without all of you. Thanks.

Most of all, we definitely want to praise our Lord Jesus Christ for our personal salvation and the incredible spirit and wisdom he has given to enrich one's life through his parables.

Finally, may God richly bless you readers as you use this book to augment your own personal study and research, so that it may guide and enrich your lives, as well as the lives of others, as you seek to serve him.

CONTENTS

Acknowledgements V

CHAPTER 1 WELCOME 1
- Introduction 2
- Styles of Speech 3
- Explanations About Parables 4
- How to Use the Parables............................ 6
- Correctly Understanding Parables 8
- About the Parables 9
- About This Book 10

CHAPTER 2 PARABLES OF THE KINGDOM OF GOD:
            NATURE AND DEVELOPMENT................. 13
- The Sower.. 14
- Wheat and Tares 19
- The Seed 27
- Mustard Seed 33
- Leaven.. 37
- Hidden Treasure 43
- Pearl 45
- Dragnet 47
- Householder 49

CHAPTER 3 PARABLES ON SALVATION 51
- Rich Fool.. 52
- Lost Sheep 61

- Lost Coin.. 64
- Lost (Prodigal) Son 66

CHAPTER 4 PARABLES OF PRAYER........................ 75
- Friend at Midnight.................................. 76
- Persistent Widow and Unjust Judge 82
- Pharisee and the Publican 89

CHAPTER 5 PARABLES OF FORGIVENESS................. 97
- Unmerciful Servant................................. 98
- Two Debtors 104

CHAPTER 6 PARABLES OF HOW TO LIVE OUR LIVES...109
- House on the Rock 110
- Good Samaritan 115
- The Good Shepherd 121

CHAPTER 7 PARABLES OF SERVICE AND REWARDS 129
- Obedient Servant 130
- Ten Pounds..136
- Vineyard Laborers 144
- Talents...150

CHAPTER 8 PARABLES OF THE NATION OF ISRAEL
        AND REJECTION OF THE MESSIAH:
        THE LAST WEEK OF JESUS' MINISTRY.....157
- New Cloth 161
- New Wine..162
- Barren Fig Tree 165
- Great Supper 171
- Two Sons 178
- Wicked Tenants......................................184
- The Fig Tree 191

CHAPTER 9   PARABLES OF THE LORD'S RETURN 197
- Watchful Servant....................................198
- Shrewd and Unjust Steward 206
- Rich Man & Lazarus 210
- Master's Return.....................................219
- Wedding Garment...................................222
- The Ten Virgins 228
- Sheep and Goats....................................234

Index..239

About the Authors 243

CHAPTER ONE

WELCOME

INTRODUCTION

STYLES OF SPEECH

EXPLANATIONS

HOW TO USE THE PARABLES

CORRECTLY UNDERSTANDING THE PARABLES

ABOUT THE PARABLES

ABOUT THIS BOOK

INTRODUCTION

When you read a book about someone famous, that biography does not cover all the details of their life. The ordinary and mundane points of a person's life is not of particular interest. Only the significant events and words they said, which also affect the lives of others, are noteworthy.

Jesus spoke in normal conversations with many people in many circumstances during his lifetime. However, not every word was recorded. Only those words, which were recorded and considered important, were documented in the Holy Bible (and in some editions, highlighted in red letters).

His words were often compassionate or comforting, angry or scolding, using teasing, humorous, or instructive teachings, as he interacted with others. He gave long sermons (the Sermon on the Mount is a wonderful example), short lessons, prayers, rebukes, encouragements, and answers to questions. His targets were groups and individuals, Jews and Gentiles, disciples and Romans, and friends and foes.

Whenever and wherever he was, all those with him had opportunities to learn from his words.

And each of us today can also read, study, learn, and apply that wisdom to our lives, no matter the format.

Some of the most profound words spoken by Jesus are his parables, which are covered in this book.

Now, as a child of God, you are able to read, study, and understand these parables, and thus have the **Keys to the Kingdom**.

STYLES OF SPEECH

Jesus had many styles of speech, not just in normal conversations, including:

1. Fable.
   An imaginary story in which animated or inanimate objects might speak and reason like human beings.

2. Simile.
   A comparison of two or more objects with the purpose of finding points of likeness or similarity. Usually using words such as "like" or "as". An example:

   > *"Ye are the salt of the earth, but if the salt have lost its savor, with what shall it be salted? It is thereafter good for nothing, but to be cast out, and to be trodden under foot of men."* (Matthew 5:13)

3. Metaphor.
   A figure of speech that describes something as though it actually is something else, thereby enhancing understanding and insight. Examples: Herod = fox, or Bread = body, Leaven = sin, or Ring = king.

4. Allegory.
   A historical reality used to represent a deeper truth, or imply a "stereo-type". A phrase like "*I AM*" could be such an indicator.

   - "*I am the door.*" (John 10:7)
   - "*I am the God of Abraham.*" (Mark 12:26)
   - "*I am the light of the world.*" (John 9:5)

5. Proverb.
   A short statement of generally accepted wisdom or truth.

6. Parable.
   Usually a story or narrative drawn from nature or human circumstances, from which a spiritual lesson can be made by comparison. Often defined as "an earthly story with a heavenly meaning." Bible scholar Warren Wiersbe's description is "*a story that places one thing beside another for the purpose of teaching.*" A parable can usually be identified by the use of the word "*as*" or "*like*".

EXPLANATIONS ABOUT PARABLES.

<u>What is a "parable"?</u>

1. It's Meaning:
   The word "parable" in the Greek is a transliteration as $\pi \alpha \rho \alpha \beta o \lambda \acute{\eta}$, and is pronounced as word "*P A R A B O L E*" (para-bow-lay). It means "*to place beside, to cast alongside*".

2. Method:
   Parables put the known next to the unknown. They use comparisons or contrasts to teach a spiritual lesson.

3. Response:
   When shared, the hearer would then be reminded of a similar circumstance in their own life, which would prompt or challenge that individual to think and make a choice, either for or against the lesson provided.

Use of Parables in the New Testament

1. The parables of Jesus Christ are used at least three dozen times in the Gospels of Matthew, Mark, and Luke, and once in the Gospel of John. There are none in the Epistles. In John 10:6, the word "parable" is used but it uses a different word which is better rendered "*proverb or figure of speech*". We will, however, examine this parable as well.
2. There are other "parables" in the Old Testament by other authors but none attributed directly to Jesus Christ.

Why did Jesus Teach in Parables?

"All these things spake Jesus unto the multitude in parables; and without a parable spake He not unto them; That it might be fulfilled which was spoken by the prophet, saying, I will open my mouth in parables; I will utter things which have been kept secret from the foundation of the world." (Matthew 13:34-35)

1. The Fulfillment of Scriptures. (Matthew 13:14). These verses are quoted five times in the New Testament.

(Matthew 13:14-15; Mark 4:12; Luke 8:10; John 12:39-40; and Acts 28:26-27).
The prophecy that refers to the spiritual deterioration of the Jewish people.
(Isaiah 6:9-10).

2. To reveal their spiritual condition. (Matthew 13:11-15).
3. To make new truths known to interested hearers. (Matthew 13:11-12; 16-17).
4. To conceal truth from disinterested hearers and rebels at heart. (Matthew 13:11-15).
5. To awaken the spiritual senses of the Jewish people.
6. To bring accountability.

An Observation.

Hearing the Word of God is not a static event, it is a dynamic experience.

We are either better or worse for hearing God's Word.

Our response determines the outcome.

(Matthew 11:20-24).

HOW TO USE THE PARABLES

How to Study Parables.

1. Study the parable in context. Spiritualizing the parable can make it teach just about anything.

2. Look for the main truth. Don't try to attach spiritual meaning to every little detail.

3. Parables illustrate doctrine; they do not define doctrine. Don't attempt to build doctrine on parables only.

4. Prayerfully ask God for spiritual understanding.

How to Apply Parables.

> "*But he that knew not, and did commit things worthy of stripes, shall be beaten with few stripes. For unto whomsoever much is given, of him shall be much required; and to whom men have committed much, of him they will ask the more.*" (Luke 12:48)

1. **Learn** the truth.
   Parables expose the thoughts of our hearts and our attitudes toward spiritual truth.

2. **Live** the truth.
   We need to be doers of the Word and not merely hearers.

   > "*But be ye doers of the Word, and not hearers only, deceiving your own selves*". (James 1:22)

3. **Share** the truth.
   Spiritual truth not used is wasted because it accomplishes nothing. If you do nothing with what you hear from this course, you have learned nothing worth knowing.

4. **Understand** the truth.
   It is important that you understand the purpose that Jesus spoke in parables, as well as to the Jews to He spoke with. Consideration must also be given to the mind of the listeners. What was important

to them can be easily lost in our cultural frame of reference. Parables are a wonderful tool our Lord used in teaching spiritual truth to the people.

CORRECTLY UNDERSTANDING PARABLES

A. **Be Logical.**

B. Keep the Big Picture in Mind. What are the main principles emphasized?

C. The Setting. Where is the parable given and to whom?

D. The Story. What is the story is about?

E. The Spiritual Message. What spiritual message is being taught?

2. **Use Common Sense.**

A. There is only one central spiritual message.

B. Some details may carry a spiritual lesson, but they always relate to the central spiritual message.

C. There may be some details that carry no spiritual significance, but they are necessary to "flesh out" the story.

Five Points for Understanding Parables.

1. Jesus spoke to his fellow Jews who were expecting a Messiah to deliver them. Most thought of this deliverance as a physical one from Roman rule rather than a spiritual one from sin.
2. The term "Kingdom of Heaven" is a description of all who claim to know God, whether saved or lost.

A clear grasp of this concept will unlock many of the parables.

3. Words that are used in the Old Testament as symbols such as "leaven" for "sin", or "light" for "righteousness"; retain their meaning in the New Testament.

4. Parables teach one main truth. Other elements may support that truth but they never negate it.

5. Some elements of the parable are necessary to "flesh out" the story but they have no significant theological meaning.

Remembering these five principles will help you as you study Jesus' parables. May they be a blessing to you as you study their truth.

ABOUT THE PARABLES

Parabolic Classifications.

1. Many different parables were spoken by Jesus and taught in the Gospels of the New Testament. There are many different topics and applications used, depending on the audience, context, and subjects.

2. The historical classification system of these New Testament parables is adapted and modified for use in this book, and was originally developed by Scottish minister and theologian Alexander B. Bruce in his eight-volume study "The Parabolic Teaching of Christ", published in London in 1904.

3. These parables are sometimes grouped in different styles and categories. They may include:

A. Didactic Parables:
Intended to convey instruction and teach a moral lesson.

B. Evangelic Parables:
Contains a spirit belonging to the doctrines of man's sinful condition and need of salvation and of God's grace.

C. Prophetic and Judicial Parables:
The administration of justice and judgment of God, pertaining to the predictions of the consequences of future events.

ABOUT THIS BOOK

1. Scripture.
All the scripture verses and references used in this study guide are quoted from the Authorized Version of the King James Bible, and are quoted in *italics* in each lesson.

2. Chapters.
The parables in each of chapters 2 through 8 of this book are grouped based on their type or category (see the previous page).

3. Lessons.
Each parable is a unique "lesson", which is broken into three parts:

A. Scripture.
The scripture verses (in *italics)* provided relates to that specific parable. While some parables may only have verses from only one Gospel, other parables may have multiple verses from

other Gospels. Only the predominant scripture will be in the lesson. However, all verses will be referred to for further reading and study.

B. Lesson.
The lesson itself will explain the actual parable, and provide the settings, circumstances, insight, people involved, and clarification to that specific parable.

C. Application.
Questions are then asked of the reader. What do you think?, What would you do? Consider this: What if Jesus was personally speaking face-to-face with you right now, what decision and/or action would you make?

Finally, it is our hope and prayer that in your studies of Christ's parables, you will be further blessed and equipped, as you seek to serve and glorify Our Lord.

CHAPTER TWO

PARABLES OF THE KINGDOM OF GOD: NATURE AND DEVELOPMENT

Lesson 2-1 The Sower   Matt 13:3-9, 18-23
                                         Mark 4:2-9, 11-20
                                         Luke 8:4-15

Lesson 2-2 Wheat and Tares   Matt 13:24-30;
                                                   36-43

Lesson 2-3 Growing Seed   Mark 4:26-29

Lesson 2-4 Mustard Seed   Matt 13:31-32
                                         Mark 4:30-32
                                         Luke 13:18-19

Lesson 2-5 Leaven   Matt 13:33
                                         Luke 13:20-21

Lesson 2-6 Hidden Treasure   Matt 13:44

Lesson 2-7 Pearl of Great Price   Matt 13:45-46

Lesson 2-8 Drag-Net   Matt 13:47-50

Lesson 2-9 Householder   Matt 13:52

Lesson 2-1

The Parable of the Sower

Matthew 13:3-9,18-23; Mark 4:3-9,11-20;
Luke 8:4-15

Matthew 13:3-9, 18-23

3 And he spoke many things unto them in parables, saying, Behold, a sower went forth to sow;

4 And when he sowed, some seeds fell by the way side, and the fowls came and devoured them up:

5 Some fell upon stony places, where they had not much earth: and forthwith they sprung up, because they had no deepness of earth:

6 And when the sun was up, they were scorched; and because they had no root, they withered away.

7 And some fell among thorns; and the thorns sprung up, and choked them:

8 But other fell into good ground, and brought forth fruit, some a hundredfold, some sixtyfold, some thirtyfold.

9 Who hath ears to hear, let him hear.

18 Hear ye therefore the parable of the sower.

19 When any one hears the word of the kingdom, and understands it not, then comes the wicked one, and catches away that which was sown in his heart. This is he which received.seed by the way side.

20 But he that received the seed into stony places, the same is he that hears the word, and anon with joy receives it;

²¹ Yet hath he not root in himself, but endures for a while: for when tribulation or persecution arises because of the word, by and by he is offended.

²² He also that received seed among the thorns is he that hears the word; and the care of this world, and the deceitfulness of riches, choke the word, and he becomes unfruitful.

²³ But he that received seed into the good ground is he that heareth the word, and understands it; which also bears fruit, and brings forth, some a hundredfold, some sixty, some thirty.

Lesson 2-1

The parable of the sower is one of the first parables that Jesus spoke. It was given after the Pharisees rejected Jesus' message and accused him of evil.

> *"This fellow doth not cast out devils, but by Beelzebub the prince of the devils."* (Matthew 12:24)

The emphasis of this parable is twofold: the seed, representing the Word of God; and the soil, representing various conditions of the heart. The sower represents Jesus, though it easily applies to everyone else, who gives out God's Word.

Let's examine the elements of this parable.

I. The **Seed.** God's Word. (vv.3-4, 18-19)
Only God's Word is capable of changing a heart and life. Outward reformation is merely window dressing and fails to address the issue of sin. Inward transformation through God's Word led by the Holy Spirit can make a man fit for heaven. God's Word is the right seed to produce salvation and fruit.

"That ye might walk worthy of the Lord unto all pleasing, being fruitful in every good work, and increasing in the knowledge of God." (Colossians 1:10)

"But grow in grace, and in the knowledge of our Lord and Savior Jesus Christ. To him be the glory both now and forever. Amen." (2 Peter 3:18)

II. The **Soil.** Human Heart. (vv.4-9, 19-23)

    A. "The **Wayward Heart.**" (v.19) "Rejected Faith". The Word of God doesn't penetrate. This particular ground is compacted and hard. Seed cannot grow there because it is unable to find a place to enter the soil. Satan's helpers, represented by the birds, takes away the seed and it doesn't grow. This is why you can talk to someone about God, and the next day they don't remember what you said.

    B. The "**Stony Heart.**" (vv.5-6, 20-21) "Convenience Faith."
In Palestine there are large limestone formations that in some places only a few inches below the soil. This obviously prevents plants from sending their roots down far enough to secure the necessary water to survive. When the weather becomes hot, the roots are killed. The plant dies because it's roots are not deep enough to sustain itself in the heat. These are people who have a superficial faith, and not a saving faith. Persecution and trials strengthen true believers and drives out false ones. This person doesn't have a saving faith but one of convenience.

"They went out from us, but they were not of us; for if they had been of us, they would no doubt have continued with us; but they went out, that they might be made manifest that they were not all of us." (1 John 2:19)

C. The "**Thorny Heart.**" (vv.7, 22) "Distracted Faith". This soil is full of competing seeds. These seeds are aggressive and like weeds. They choke the good seed until they destroy it. This person allows God to take a backseat in their life. His heart is one that is unfruitful because of the cares of this world, the deceitfulness of riches, the lust of things (Mark 4:19) and the pleasure of life (Luke 8:14). The word cares means "worries" or "anxieties". These shallow professors of faith may or may not be saved. They show no evidence in their life and are at best carnal Christians. They have failed to make a clean break with the world.

D. The "**Good Heart.**" (vv.8-9, 23) "Applied Faith." The evidence of having a good heart is in the response to God's word.

1. While a good heart hears and **responds** to God's Word, the results may vary: *"a hundred fold, some sixty fold, some thirty fold"* (v.23)
2. Every good heart **hears** God's Word, **understands it**, and **obeys** it.
3. Every good heart will be **fruitful**.
Only God knows your heart. Is it planted in God's Word? Or, is it hard, unresponsive, and focused on the world, rather than God?

Lesson 2-1
Application

1. What kind of heart do you have?

2. How do you know?

3. Name the last time you heard a Bible principle that you applied?

4. Examine Galatians 5:18-26.

   What fruits are evident in your life?

5. Are You a Sower of God's Word?

Lesson 2-2

Parable of Wheats and Tares

Matthew 13:24-30, 36-43

Matthew 13:24-30, 36-43

24 *Another parable he put forth unto them, saying, The kingdom of heaven is likened unto a man which sowed good seed in his field:*

25 *But while men slept, his enemy came and sowed tares among the wheat, and went his way.*

26 *But when the blade was sprung up, and brought forth fruit, then appeared the tares also.*

27 *So the servants of the householder came and said unto him, Sir, didst not thou sow good seed in thy field? from whence then hath it tares?*

28 *He said unto them, An enemy hath done this. The servants said unto him, Will you then that we go and gather them up?*

29 *But he said, Nay; lest while ye gather up the tares, ye root up also the wheat with them.*

30 *Let both grow together until the harvest: and in the time of harvest I will say to the reapers, Gather ye together first the tares, and bind them in bundles to burn them: but gather the wheat into my barn.*

36 *Then Jesus sent the multitude away, and went into the house: and his disciples came unto him, saying, Declare unto us the parable of the tares of the field.*

37 *He answered and said unto them, He that sows the good seed is the Son of man;*

38 The field is the world; the good seed are the children of the kingdom; but the tares are the children of the wicked one;

39 The enemy that sowed them is the devil; the harvest is the end of the world; and the reapers are the angels.

40 As therefore the tares are gathered and burned in the fire; so shall it be in the end of this world.

41 The Son of man shall send forth his angels, and they shall gather out of his kingdom all things that offend, and them which do iniquity;

42 And shall cast them into a furnace of fire: there shall be wailing and gnashing of teeth.

43 Then shall the righteous shine forth as the sun in the kingdom of their Father. Who hath ears to hear, let him hear.

Lesson 2-2

I. The Setting.

    A. A continuation of Teaching about the Kingdom of Heaven.

    B. Given to Disciples and Multitudes.

II. The Story. "Good seed in field, corrupted by bad seed". Wheat was considered the most important grain in biblical times. The other grains, barley and flax were lesser in value. Tares or bearded darnel are a poisonous grass which is undistinguishable from wheat when they grow side by side. At harvest time the black grains of darnel are smaller, fewer and hence lighter. They remain head up. The wheat stalk is bent over from its load. They can then be distinguished from each other.

Eating darnel can produce nausea, convulsions, diarrhea, and sometimes death. It is a fitting picture of false doctrine.

In this parable, the sower is Jesus Christ. The enemy who sowed the tares is Satan. The wheat represents those who are saved and the tares represent those who appear to be saved but are lost. At the time of judgment, the saved-wheat will be gathered into the barn-heaven. The lost-tares will be judged and cast into the fire.

A. Man (Sowers). Christ. (v.37)

B. Seed. Believers. (v.38)

C. Field. World. (v.38)

D. Tares. Unbelievers. (v.38)

E. Enemy. Satan. (39)

F. Reapers. Angels. (v.39)

G. Harvest. End of the age. (v.39)

III. Two different **Sowers** and their seed.

A. **Jesus Christ**.
His seed is good and beneficial to humankind. It produces salvation and righteous living.

B. **Satan.**
His seed is an imitation of God's. It looks similar but produces death and judgment.
Both Christ and Satan are still sowing seed today. Christ's seed is the Word of God. Satan's seed is the perversion of the Word of God. Have you received the Word of God and accepted Jesus as your Savior? It is possible to teach a Bible class,

serve on a committee, be a church officer, come regularly to worship, give and sing in the choir and still be lost and end up in hell. Some may think they are wheat, but they are tares.

IV. Observations concerning the **Seed**.

    A. Whenever **Christ** plants true believers, Satan plants false believers who oppose the Word and hinder the harvest.

    B. The **Kingdom of Heaven** is a picture of all of who claim to believe, a combination of true seed (believers) and false seed (children of the devil).

    C. There is confusion about the crop from the seed. (vv.27-28)
    The farmer's servants were confused about what had happened. Their lack of watchfulness allowed the enemy to corrupt the field with bad seed.

V. Some verses which Contrast **Good Seed** and **Bad Seed**.

    A. The **Good Seed.**

        1. **Adam and Eve's offspring.**

> *"And I will put enmity between thee and the woman, and between thy seed and her seed. It shall bruise thy head, and thou shalt bruise his heel".*
> (Genesis 3:15)

KEYS TO THE KINGDOM

2. **Cain and Abel.** (Genesis 4)

> *"Not as Cain, who was of that wicked one, and slew his brother. And wherefore slew he him? Because his own works were evil, and his brother's righteous."* (1 John 3:12)

3. **Abraham.**

> *"Now to Abraham and his seed were the promises made. He saith not, And to seeds, as of many; but as of one, and to thy seed, which is Christ."* (Galatians 3:16)

4. **Christ.**

> *"But when the fullness of the time was come, God sent forth his Son, made of a woman, made under the law."* (Galatians 4:4)

5. **Believers.**

> *"But other fell into good ground, and brought forth fruit, some an hundredfold, some sixtyfold, some thirtyfold."* (Matthew 13:8)

B. The **Bad Seed.**

1. **False Message.**

> *"I marvel that ye are so soon removed from him that called you into the grace of Christ unto another gospel."* (Galatians 1:6)

2. **False Ministers.**

"For such are false apostles, deceitful workers, transforming themselves into the apostles of Christ. And no marvel; for Satan himself is transformed into an angel of light. Therefore it is no great thing if his ministers also be transformed as the ministers of righteousness; whose nd shall be according to their works." (2 Corinthians 11:13-15)

3. **False Righteousness.**

"For I bear them record that they have a zeal of God, but not according to knowledge. For they being ignorant of God's righteousness, and going about to establish their own righteousness, have not submitted themselves unto the righteousness of God." (Romans 10:2-3)

4. **False Brethren.**

"in perils among false brethren." (2 Corinthians 11:26)

VI. The **Harvest** of the Seed.

No one plants seed without expecting a harvest. Revelation 14:14-16 tells of God's time of harvest.

> "And I looked, and behold a white cloud, and upon the cloud one sat like unto the Son of man, having on his head a golden crown, and in his hand a sharp sickle. And another angel came out of the temple crying with a loud voice to him that sat on the cloud. Thrust in thy sickle, and reap: for the time is come for thee to reap: for the harvest of the earth is ripe. And he that sat on the cloud thrust in his sickle on the earth; and the earth was reaped."

Some are good seed. Some are bad seed. Bad seed may not even know that they are bad. At the time of harvest, God will sort through and separate the good from the bad. Are you good seed? Is Jesus Christ your Savior? If not, the Lake of Fire awaits. Make sure you know Jesus as your Savior.

Lesson 2-2
Application

1. What does it mean "while men slept"?

2. How do you tell "good seed" from "bad seed"?

3. Why are the servants not told to dislodge the tares?

4. What should be your response to tares?

5. What will happen to the wheat and the tares?

LESSON 2-3

THE PARABLE OF THE GROWING SEED

Mark 4:26-29

Mark 4:26-29

26 *And he said, So is the kingdom of God, as if a man should cast seed into the ground;*

27 *And should sleep, and rise night and day, and the seed should spring and grow up, he knows not how.*

28 *For the earth bringeth forth fruit of herself; first the blade, then the ear, after that the full corn in the ear.*

29 *But when the fruit is brought forth, immediately he puts in the sickle, because the harvest is come.*

Lesson 2-3

I. The **Setting.**

    A. After the Parable of the Sower (Matthew 13:3-9, 18-23). [see LESSON 2-1]

    B. Jesus taught this parable while he was alone with His disciples. (v.10)

    C. The man who *"casts seed into the ground"*. (v.26), is, of course, Jesus Christ. What can we learn about growth in the Kingdom of God?

II. The **Story**. *"a man cast seed into the ground"*. (v.26)

    A. Man. Christ.

    B. Seed. Word of God.

C. Sleep and rise. Passing of time.

D. Growth. Kingdom of God.

    1. Blade. beginning.
    2. Ear. middle.
    3. Full corn. completion.
       The word "corn" in the Bible is a generic word which means grain.

> *"Verily, verily, I say unto you, Except a corn of wheat fall into the ground and die, it abideth alone; but if it die, it bringeth forth much fruit."* (John 12:24)

E. Harvest. Judgment.

III.   **Sleep** and Rise. Passing of Time.

There can be **no growth** without seed. (v.26). This suggests that we also have responsibility.

A. God's Word must be **given out**.

"And the fruit of righteousness is sown in peace of them that make peace". (James 3:18)

"So then faith cometh by hearing, and hearing by the Word of God." (Romans 10:17)

B. God's Word will accomplish **God's will**.
God's word is not dependent on man to accomplish God's will.

> *"So shall My word be that goeth forth out of My mouth; it shall not return unto Me void, but it shall*

accomplish that which I please and it shall prosper in the thing whereto I sent it." (Isaiah 55:11)

C. God's Word is **not dependent** on man to accomplish God's will. We can sow, but we cannot make the seed sprout. That is God's domain.

IV. Growth is **slow**, but over time will show. (v.27).

A. We may not understand what God is doing, but we must believe that He is working.

B. This concept of not knowing or understanding how **God is working** is common in s**cripture**.

"As thou knowest not what is the way of the spirit, nor how the bones do grow in the womb of her that is with child: even so thou knowest not the works of God who maketh all." (Ecclesiastes 11:5)

"For my thoughts are not your thoughts, neither are your ways my ways, saith the Lord. For as the heavens are higher than the earth, so are my ways higher than your ways, and my thoughts than your thoughts." (Isaiah 55:8-9)

C. God is never late but always on time.

"But when the fullness of the time was come, God sent forth His Son, made of a woman, made under the law." (Galatians 4:4)

D. When God comes, there will be a time of harvest (judgment).

V. Growth follows a pattern, (v.28).

A. **Blade.** the beginning.
When the crop first sprouts out of the ground.

B. **Ear.** the middle.
When the crop is identified by its fruit that it bares.

C. **Full corn.** the completion.
When the crop is ready to be harvested.
The word "corn" in the Bible is a generic word that means grain.

> *"Verily, verily, I say unto you, except a corn of wheat fall into the ground and die, it abideth alone: but if it die, it bringeth forth much fruit."* (John 12:24)

The ancient Bible lands did not have "corn", a New World grain.

VI. Growth leads to a **Harvest**, (v.29)

> *And let us not be weary in well doing: for in due season we shall reap, if we faint not."* (Galatians 6:9)

While the harvest seems to be far away, eventually it will come.

> *"And another angel came out of the temple, crying with a loud voice to him that sat on the cloud. Thrust in thy sickle, and reap: for the time is come for thee to reap: for the harvest of the*

earth is ripe. And he that sat on the cloud thrust in his sickle on the earth; and the earth was reaped." (Revelation 14:15-16)

A couple of years ago, seed was recovered from an Egyptian tomb that had been sealed in a vessel. Thousands of years old, when it was recently planted, it grew!

"Being born again, not of corruptible seed, but of incorruptible, by the word of God, which liveth and abideth forever." (1 Peter 1:23)

"For the word of God is quick (living) and powerful,.." (Hebrews 4:12)

God's Word changes lives. It brings salvation. Let us do our part to give out God's word. Tell others about Jesus. Leave tracts. Invite others to hear God's Word. Let's help to plant seeds and watch God's kingdom grow.

"For as the earth bringeth forth her bud, and as the garden causeth the things that are sown in it to spring forth; so the Lord God will cause righteousness and praise to spring forth before all the nations." (Isaiah 61:11)

Lesson 2-3
Application

1. Do we have a responsibility to sow the seed? (Word of God)

2. Do you have a regular time when you sow God's Word?

3. How do you plan to accomplish sowing God's Word?

4. Is the Word of God limited by our ability?

Lesson 2-4

Parable of the Mustard Seed

*"The tree grew, and was strong, and
the height thereof reached unto heaven"*

Matthew 13:30-32; Mark 4:30-33;
Luke 13:18-19

Mark 4:30-33

*30 And he said, To what shall we liken the kingdom of
God? Or with what comparison shall we compare it?*
*31 It is like a grain of mustard seed, which, when it is
sown in the earth, is less than all the seeds that be
in the earth:*
*32 But when it is sown, it grows up, and becometh greater
than all herbs, and shoots out great branches; so that
the fowls of the air may lodge under the shadow of it.*
*33 And with many such parables spoke he the word unto
them, as they were able to hear it.*

Lesson 2-4

I. The **Setting.**

  A. A continuation of the Teaching about the Kingdom
     of Heaven.

  B. Given to the Disciples and Multitudes.

II. The **Story.** "The Mustard Seed."

The black mustard seed is about the size of a pin head. It is grown for oil as well as seasoning. It can reach a height of more than 15 feet. Its flowers are yellow.

III. Growth of the Mustard Seed.

A. Sudden at first, it slows at the end of the age. This suggests abnormal growth and expansion. There are many branches of Christendom, but some are dead. Christendom has become a worldwide power of untold wealth and political power.

B. Trees, represent world power

> "and the sight thereof to the end of all the earth." (Daniel 4:11) (Nebuchadnezzar)

IV. Place Where Evil Resides.

A. Birds in the parable of the sower [see lessons 2-1 and 2-2] are seen as a symbol of Satan and his helpers:

> "And when he sowed, some seeds fell by the way side, and the fowls came and devoured them up." (Matthew 13:4)

> "When any one heareth the word of the kingdom, and understandeth it not, then cometh the wicked one, and catcheth away that which was sown in his heart. This is he which received seed by the way side." (Matthew 13:19)

B. The church will be a resting place for Satan to find refuge. He and his helpers will seek to corrupt the church from within.

C. An example is Paul's admonition to the elders of Ephesus.

> *"For I know this, that after my departing shall grievous wolves enter in among you, not sparing the flock. Also of your own selves shall men arise, speaking perverse things, to draw away disciples after them."* (Acts 20:29-30)

The church will be a resting place for Satan to find refuge. He and his helpers will seek to corrupt the church from within.

Lesson 2-4
Application

1. Why do you believe that the church grew rapidly at first, but slows down at the end of the age?

2. Why do unbelievers seek positions in the church?

3. How can we prevent Satan from infecting a church?

4. What are you doing to help the church grow?

LESSON 2-5

PARABLE OF THE LEAVEN

Matthew 13:33; Luke 13:20-21

Luke 13:20-21

20 And again he said, Whereunto shall I liken the kingdom of God?

21 It is like leaven, which a woman took and hid in three measures of meal, till the whole was leavened.

Lesson 2-5

I. The Setting.

    A. A continuation of the teaching of the Kingdom of Heaven.
Note : Luke 13:20-21 calls it the "Kingdom of God".

    B. Given to the Disciples and Multitudes.

II. The Story. "The leaven permeates the whole loaf."

    A. Leaven's usage is **limited**.

        1. Excluded from the **Passover.**

> *"And the people took their dough before it was leavened, their kneading troughs being bound up in their clothes upon their shoulders."* (Exodus 12:34)

2. Excluded from **Sacrifice**

> *"No meat offering, which ye shall bring unto the Lord, shall be made with leaven; for ye shall burn no leaven, nor any honey, in any offering of the Lord made by fire."* (Leviticus 2:11)

B. Used throughout the Bible as a symbol of **evil**.

1. **Hypocrisy.**

> *"In the meantime, when there were gathered together an innumerable multitude of people; insomuch that they trode one upon another, he began to say unto his disciples first of all, Beware ye of the leaven of the Pharisees, which is hypocrisy."* (Luke 12:1)

2. **False Doctrine.**

> *"Then Jesus said unto them, Take heed and beware of the leaven of the Pharisees and of the Sadducees. And they reasoned among themselves saying, It is because we have taken no bread. Which when Jesus perceived, he said unto them, O ye of little faith, why reason ye among yourselves, because ye have brought no bread? Do ye not yet understand, neither remember the five loaves of the five thousand, and how many*

baskets ye took up? Neither the seven loaves of the four thousand, and how many baskets ye took up? How is it that ye do not understand that I spake it not to you concerning bread, that ye should beware of the leaven of the Pharisees and of the Sadducees? Then understood they how he bade them not beware of the leaven of bread, but of the doctrine of the Pharisees and of the Sadducees." (Matthew 16:6-12)

3. **Pride.**

"And ye are puffed up, and have not rather mourned, that he that hath done this deed might be taken away from you." 1 Corinthians 5:5-8, "To deliver such an one unto Satan for the destruction of the flesh, that the spirit may be saved in the day of the Lord Jesus. Your glorying is not good. Know ye not that a little leaven leaventh the whole lump? Purge out therefore the old leaven, that ye may be a new lump, as ye are unleavened. For even Christ our Passover is sacrificed for us. Therefore let us keep the feast, not with old leaven, neither with the leaven of malice and wickedness; but with the unleavened bread of sincerity and truth." (1 Corinthians 5:2)

C. **Hidden** is secret.

Leaven grows from within. False doctrine and sin often grow undetected until the damage is done.

D. Some final observations about leaven:

1. It grows **quickly.**
2. It grows **quietly**.
3. It corrupts **completely**.

Many schools and churches that once proclaimed the Gospel have turned from the truth and promote error. False doctrine and sin must be confronted before they establish themselves and destroys God's work.

Lesson 2-5
Application

1. How can leaven affect your school or church, or your life?

2. How do you know?

3. In what ways can you deal with the problem you have found?

4. How does leaven destroy Christian churches, schools?

and organizations ?

LESSONS ON THE PARABLES
OF HIDDEN TREASURES

Lesson 2-6   In The Field   Matt 13:44

Lesson 2-7   Pearl of Great Price   Matt 13:45-46

Lesson 2-8   Drag-Net   Matt 13:47-50

Lesson 2-9   Householder   Matt 13:51-52

At the end of the age, God will deal with four chosen groups of people:

1. The **Jews**. represented by the hidden treasure,
2. The **church**. represented by the pearl,
3. The **saved Gentiles**. represented by those separated and saved from the dragnet, and,
4. The **householder**. (a scholar in both Old and New Testaments.)

Since these parables are connected, we will look at them as a unit. These were told to his disciples, the multitude being sent away.
(Matthew.13:36).

Let's look at these parables:

LESSON 2-6

THE PARABLE OF THE HIDDEN TREASURE

Matthew 13:44

Matthew 13:44

Again, the kingdom of heaven is like unto treasure hid in a field; the which when a man hath found, he hides, and for joy thereof goes and sells all that he hath, and buys that field. (Matthew 13:44)

Lesson 2-6

I. The Story. **"The Hidden Treasure."** (v.44) Israel.

    A. A common interpretation of this parable is that the sinner finds salvation in Jesus and gives up all that he possesses to gain that salvation.

    B. Problems with this interpretation

        1. No one has ever given up all that they possess for salvation except Christ. Neither you nor I can give up anything we have to obtain salvation. Salvation is by God's grace *through* **Jesus Christ.**

> *"For by grace are you saved and that not of yourselves. It is the gift of God, not of works lest any man should boast".* (Ephesians 2:8-9)

2. Jesus Christ is not a **hidden treasure**. He is the best-known person of history.
3. **No sinner** ever found Christ.

> "*Having the understanding darkened, being alienated from the life of God through the ignorance that is in them because of the blindness of their heart*". (Ephesians 4:18)

4. The **man did not purchase** the treasure, but rather the field.

> "*the field is the world*". (Matthew 13:38)

C. An Old Testament Consideration.

1. In the Old Testament Israel is called God's treasure

> "*Now therefore if ye will obey my voice indeed, and keep my covenant, then ye shall be a peculiar treasure unto me above all people: for all the earth is mine*". (Exodus 19:5)

2. Israel should have been a witness, but it failed to accept Christ and witness God's grace. The Messiah died for the world and also in a special way for Israel.

Lesson 2-7

The Pearl of Great Price

Matthew 13:45-46

Matthew 13:45-46

45 Again, the kingdom of heaven is like unto a merchant man, seeking goodly pearls:
46 Who, when he had found one pearl of great price, went and sold all that he had, and bought it.

Lesson 2-7

I. The Story. "The Pearl of Great Price."
    (v.45-46) The Church.

   A. The pearl represents the church.

      1. The merchant is Christ.
      2. A pearl grows slowly and unseen.

   B. Goodly Pearls. Christians.

   C. Pearl of Great price. Church.

      1. A pearl grows slowly and unseen.
      2. It is a product of suffering. Sand gets in and is covered by secretion

         "Christ died for the church".
         (Ephesians 5:25)

      3. Unlike other gems, a pearl represents unity. It cannot be cut or carved like other gems.

D. Practical Understanding.
   Jesus loved us and died for us that we might have eternal life.

> "*Even as Christ also loved the church, and gave Himself for it*" (Ephesians 5:25)

LESSON 2-8

PARABLE OF THE DRAG-NET

Matthew 13:47-50

Matthew 13:47-50

47 Again, the kingdom of heaven is like unto a net, that was cast into the sea, and gathered of every kind:

48 Which, when it was full, they drew to shore, and sat down, and gathered the good into vessels, but cast the bad away.

49 So shall it be at the end of the world: the angels shall come forth, and sever the wicked from among the just,

50 And shall cast them into the furnace of fire: there shall be wailing and gnashing of teeth.

Lesson 2-8

I. The Story.
    "The Dragnet cast into the sea." (vv.47-50)
    (Saved Gentiles).

   A. Net. God's gathering.

   B. Sea. World.

   C. Good Fish. Saved.

   D. Bad Fish. Cast away.

   E. Separators. Angels.

   F. The Interpretation.

The Gospel does not save everyone in the world. At the end of the world God's angels will separate the saved from the unsaved. (v.49)

> "*When the son of man shall come in His glory, and all the holy angels with Him, then shall He sit upon the throne of His glory. And before Him shall be gathered all nations and He shall separate them one from another as a shepherd divideth his sheep from the goats.*" (Matthew 25:31-32)

A. The **good fish** are placed into **vessels**.
This is a picture of the saved.

B. The **bad fish** are cast away to be **burned.**
This pictures the lost who end up being judged.

C. The sea is the **world**.
The angels will separate the saved from the lost. The lost will be cast into the fire, and there will be wailing.

LESSON 2-9

THE PARABLE OF THE HOUSEHOLDER

Matthew 13:52

Matthew 13:52

52 *Then said he unto them, Therefore, every scribe which is instructed unto the kingdom of heaven is like unto a man that is an householder, which brings forth out of his treasure things new and old.*

Lesson 2-9

I. When one understands the instruction of the Kingdom teachings, he is like a scribe (scholar) and can handle both new and old treasure from God's Word.

II. **The Conclusion of the These Parables.** (v.51-56)

1. Jesus *"Have ye understood all these things?"* (v.51)
2. The Parables draw on both old and new things. Understanding equals = Responsibility
3. Christ wants us to understand and respond to his Word with obedience.
4. Instruction completes training on the kingdom, its growth, and its development.

Lessons 2-6, 2-7, 2-8, 2-9
Applications

1. Can you tell whether someone is saved or not?

2. If you had to judge someone's salvation, how would you do it?

3. What does God expect us to do when we understand what the scriptures teach?

CHAPTER THREE

PARABLES ON SALVATION

Lesson 3-1   Rich Fool   Luke 12:16-21

The Lost

Lesson 3-2   Lost Sheep   Matt 18:11-14-15
                            Luke 15:3-7

Lesson 3-3   Lost Coin   Luke 15:8-10

Lesson 3-4   Lost Son   Luke 15:11-32
             (Prodigal)

Lesson 3-1

Parable of the Rich Fool

Luke 12:16-21

Luke 12:16-21

¹⁶ And he spoke a parable to them, saying, The ground of a certain rich man brought forth plentifully:

¹⁷ And he thought within himself, saying, What shall I do, because I have no room where to bestow my fruits?

¹⁸ And he said, This will I do: I will pull down my barns, and build greater; and there will I bestow all my fruits and my goods.

¹⁹ And I will say to my soul, Soul, you have much goods laid up for many years; take your ease, eat, drink, and be merry.

²⁰ But God said unto him, Thou fool, this night thy soul shall be required of thee: then whose shall those things be, which thou hast provided?

²¹ So is he that lays up treasure for himself, and is not rich toward God.

Lesson 3-1

It was not unusual for rabbis to be asked to settle legal matters. Rabbis were expected to help, yet Jesus declined to get involved. The problem was not the inheritance but the covetousness in these two brothers' hearts. Like many people today, they want Jesus to serve them, not save them.

Covetousness is an unquenchable fire that can never be satisfied.

> *"But seek ye first the Kingdom of God, and His righteousness: and all these things shall be added unto you."* (Matthew 6:33)

God promises to supply our needs, not our lusts.

To help his listeners understand the dangers of covetousness, Jesus gave the parable of the rich farmer.

I. The Setting.

    A. After condemning the lack of faith and hypocrisy of the scribes and Pharisees. (Luke 11:53-54)

    B. While surrounded by an innumerable multitude. (v.1)

    C. Addressed to his disciples. (v.1)

    D. After questioned about dividing an inheritance. (v.13)

    E. *"The ground of a certain rich man brought forth plentifully."* (v.16)

II. The Farmer's **Dilemma.** Too Much Wealth. (vv.15-17) What caused his dilemma?

    A. He was **materially** blessed.
I doubt that any of his neighbors thought he was a fool. In fact, I'm sure they thought of him as a smart man. They may have even been jealous of his success. Too much wealth. Bill Gates' billions of dollars. If you inherited wealth, would it create a problem for you? Would you praise God and ask him what He wanted you to do with it?
Do you say, *"I wish I had that problem?"*

B. He was **spiritually** blind. (v.15)
The wrong philosophy of wealth destroys instead of blesses.

> "give me neither poverty nor riches; feed me with food convenient for me: Lest I be full and deny thee and say, Who is the Lord? Or lest I be poor and steal, and take the name of my God in vain." (Proverbs 30:8-9)

1. Wealth can choke God's Word.

> "he that heareth the word and the care of this world and the deceitfulness of riches, choke the word, and he becometh unfruitful." (Matthew 13:22)

It may also create snares and temptations:

> "But godliness with contentment is great gain." "But they that will be rich fall into temptation and a snare, and into many foolish and hurtful lusts, which drown men in destruction and perdition."
> (1 Timothy 6:6,9)

2. It may also give you a false sense of security.

> "There is no man that hath power over the spirit to retain the spirit; neither hath he power in the day of death; and there is no discharge in that war; neither shall wickedness deliver those that are given to it."
> (Ecclesiastes 8:8)

People who are satisfied with the things money can buy are in danger of losing the things money cannot buy. This present life is not what is important.

C. The Farmer's **Delusion**. (vv.17-21)
He thought only of the **present**. Note the word "I". (vv.17-19) There is nothing wrong in saving some money.

> "There is treasure to be desired and oil in the dwelling of the wise; but a foolish man spendeth it up." (Proverbs 21:20)

But there is everything wrong when the present is honored and God is forgotten. Take care of number one is a poor philosophy to live and die by.

1. **Success.** more than enough.
2. **Satisfaction.** Eat, drink, and be merry.
3. **Security.** Goods laid up for many years.

D. He gave no thought for **eternity**, (vv.19-21)
The Epicurean Philosophy was, "Eat, drink and be merry for tomorrow we die". He had success, satisfaction and security. He thought that life came from accumulating things and that death was far away.

III. The Farmer's **Disappointment.** (vv.20-21)

A. He missed God's best in **this life**.

> "I am come that they might have life and that they might have it more abundantly." (John 10:10)

Anyone who doesn't know God has missed God's best. They can never answer, Why am I here? Where am I going? How do I get there?

B. He missed God's best in the **hereafter**. (vv.20-21)
No one who misses salvation through Christ is ready to die.

> *"For whosoever will save his life shall lose it: and whosoever will lose his life for my sake shall find it. For what is a man profited, if he shall gain the whole world, and lose his own soul? Or what shall a man give in exchange for his soul?"*
> (Matthew 16:25-26)

Some say, "I'd never sell my soul!" However, Judas sold his for thirty pieces of silver. People sell out cheap.

IV. The Farmer's **Discomfort.** The Words of the Savior. (vv.20-21)

A. Thou **fool**. (v.20)
When God calls you a fool, you are one.

B. Your **soul** is required, (v.20)

> *"And as it is appointed unto men once to die, but after this the judgment."*
> (Hebrews 9:27)

C. Riches cannot **help** you, (vv.20-21)

> *"then a great ransom cannot deliver thee. Will he esteem thy riches? No, not gold, nor all the forces of strength."*
> (Job 36:18-19)

D. Your wealth will be left **to others**. (v.20)

> "*There is an evil which I have seen under the sun, and it is common among men: A man whom God hath given riches, wealth, and honor, so that he wanteth nothing for his soul of all that he desireth, yet God giveth him not power to eat thereof, but a stranger eateth it: this is vanity, and it is an evil disease.*" (Ecclesiastes 6:1-2)

V. The farmer's **dismay.** He really had nothing, (v.21) What does it mean to be rich toward God? It means to be rich in spiritual things. How tragic when people are rich in this life but poor in the next.

Lesson 3-1
Application

1. What did this rich farmer really have?

2. Why do you think that rich people often fail to consider eternal matters?

3. What should be our attitude toward our wealth?

4. Is it a sin to be wealthy?

5. What can you do with your wealth to advance the Kingdom of God?

Lessons 3-2, 3-3, 3-4

The Parables of the Lost Sheep, Lost Coin, and Lost Son

I. The Setting.

   A. After a call for discipleship. (Luke 14:25-35)

   B. After publicans and sinners came to hear him.

   C. After murmuring of the Pharisees and Scribes

Jesus' ministry extended beyond the average citizen to the outcast and social misfit.

> *"For the Son of Man is come to save that which was lost."* (Matthew 18:11)

As the Savior's heart is toward the lost, so must our heart be, if we are to be faithful to the Great Commission.

> *"Go ye therefore and teach all nations, baptizing them in the name of the Father, and of the Son and of the Holy Ghost."* (Matthew 28:19)

The Pharisees and Scribes murmured against Christ because his compassion to outcasts was offensive to their self-righteousness.

II. The Self Righteousness of the Pharisees. (vv.1-2)

A. The people of their contempt.

1. Sinners: A class of people written off by the religious leaders of the day.
2. Publicans : Tax collectors for Rome.

B. The murmuring against others.
This attitude was quite common. They thought themselves better than others.

> *"Why do ye eat and drink with publicans and sinners?"* (Luke 5:30)

> *"God, I thank thee, that I am not as other men are, extortioners, unjust, adulterers or even as this publican."* (Luke 18:11)

In order to deal with this attitude of self-righteousness, Jesus gave the following parables (lessons):

The Lost Sheep.	3-2
The Lost Coin.	3-3
The Lost (Prodigal) Son.	3-4

LESSON 3-2

THE PARABLE OF THE LOST SHEEP

Matthew 18:11-14; Luke 15:3-7

Luke 15:3-7

³ And he spoke this parable unto them, saying,

⁴ What man of you, having an hundred sheep, if he loses one of them, doth not leave the ninety and nine in the wilderness, and go after that which is lost, until he find it?

⁵ And when he hath found it, he lays it on his shoulders, rejoicing.

⁶ And when he comes home, he calls together his friends and neighbors, saying unto them, Rejoice with me; for I have found my sheep which was lost.

⁷ I say unto you, that likewise joy shall be in heaven over one sinner that repents, more than over ninety and nine just persons, which need no repentance.

Lesson 3-2

I. The Story. *"having an hundred sheep if he lose one"*. (Luke 15:4-7)

    A. Sheep. People.

    B. Shepherd. God.

II. What Can We Learn from This Parable?

A. The Shepherd **cares** for the sheep.

> "I am the good shepherd: the good shepherd giveth his life for the sheep, But he that is a hireling and not the shepherd, whose own the sheep are not seeth the wolf coming and leaveth the sheep, and fleeth; and the wolf catcheth them and scattereth the sheep. The hireling fleeth because he is a hireling and careth not for the sheep."
> (John 10:11-13)

B. One sheep is **worth** the **effort**.
Remember, we are in the ministry of restoration. Our goal is not to humiliate but to restore a person to a right relationship to God and his fellow man.

> "For what is a man profited if he shall gain the whole world and lose his own soul? Or what shall a man give in exchange for his soul?" (Matthew 16:26)

That drunkard, the immoral, the homeless, the mentally ill, all are worthy of salvation. A sheep may not even know it is lost.

C. One sheep saved **brings** great **rejoicing** . (Luke 15:7)
The joy of a shepherd finding a lost sheep is nothing compared to the joy in heaven over one lost sheep (person saved).

Matthew 18:11-14 gives a parable about the lost sheep.

> *"Even so it is not the will of your Father which is in heaven, that one of these little ones should perish."* (v.14)

Our ministry is one of restoration.

Lesson 3-3

Parable of the Lost Coin

Luke 15:8-10

Luke 15:8-10

⁸ Either what woman having ten pieces of silver, if she lose one piece, does not light a candle, and sweep the house, and seek diligently till she find it?

⁹ And when she has found it, she called her friends and her neighbors together, saying, Rejoice with me; for I have found the piece which I had lost.

¹⁰ Likewise, I say unto you, here is joy in the presence of the angels of God over one sinner that repents.

Lesson 3-3

I. The Story. The Lost Coin.

> "*Woman having ten pieces of silver, if she loses one*". (Luke 15:8-10)

A. The **value** of the silver coin was a little more than one day's wage. The drachma was slightly smaller than a quarter, and was worth one fifth of an ox.

B. Losing a drachma was a serious reversal for a poor family household. Most houses were dimly lit by one or two small windows, and usually had dirt floors.

C. The **symbolism** of the silver coin often worn in a ten-piece garland by women representing betrothal or the marriage relationship. It is like losing your wedding ring. These coins were worn upon the brow.

D. The **rejoicing** of finding the silver coin. (vv.9-10) Note the desire to rejoice with others. Similar to the joy in heaven over one lost sinner coming to God.

Jesus' ministry was concerned with restoration.

In the story of the woman taken in adultery, and Jesus said

"He that is without sin among you, let him first cast a stone at her." (John 8:7)

After the scribes and Pharisees left, he asked:

"Woman where are those thine accusers? Hath no man condemned thee?" (v.10)

Finally, *"Neither do I condemn thee: go, and sin no more."* (verse 11)

The ministry is about people. Don't lose sight over what is important.

An observation: The coin, being metal, didn't know it was lost.

Lesson 3-4

Parable of the Lost (Prodigal) Son

Luke 15:11-32

Luke 15:11-32

¹¹ *And he said, A certain man had two sons:*

¹² *And the younger of them said to his father, Father, give me the portion of goods that fall to me. And he divided unto them his living.*

¹³ *And not many days after the younger son gathered all together, and took his journey into a far country, and there wasted his substance with riotous living.*

¹⁴ *And when he had spent all, there arose a mighty famine in that land; and he began to be in want.*

¹⁵ *And he went and joined himself to a citizen of that country; and he sent him into his fields to feed swine.*

¹⁶ *And he would fain have filled his belly with the husks that the swine did eat: and no man gave to him.*

¹⁷ *And when he came to himself, he said, How many hired servants of my father's have bread enough and to spare, and I perish with hunger!*

¹⁸ *I will arise and go to my father, and will say unto him, Father, I have sinned against heaven, and before you,*

¹⁹ *And am no more worthy to be called your son: make me as one of your hired servants.*

²⁰ *And he arose, and came to his father. But when he was yet a great way off, his father saw him, and*

had compassion, and ran, and fell on his neck, and kissed him.

21 And the son said unto him, Father, I have sinned against heaven, and in your sight, and am no more worthy to be called thy son.

22 But the father said to his servants, Bring forth the best robe, and put it on him; and put a ring on his hand, and shoes on his feet:

23 And bring here the fatted calf, and kill it; and let us eat, and be merry:

24 For this my son was dead, and is alive again; he was lost, and is found. And they began to be merry.

25 Now his elder son was in the field: and as he came and drew near to the house, he heard music and dancing.

26 And he called one of the servants, and asked what these things meant.

27 And he said unto him, Thy brother is come; and thy father has killed the fatted calf, because he has received him safe and sound.

28 And he was angry, and would not go in: therefore came his father out, and intreated him.

29 And he answering said to his father, Lo, these many years do I serve you, neither transgressed I at any time thy commandment: and yet you never gave me a kid, that I might make merry with my friends:

30 But as soon as this thy son was come, which has devoured his living with harlots, you have killed for him the fatted calf.

31 And he said unto him, Son, you art ever with me, and all that I have is yours.

32 It was meet that we should make merry, and be glad: for this your brother was dead, and is alive again; and was lost, and is found.

Lesson 3-4

In Luke 15:2, the Pharisees and Scribes murmured because Jesus received sinners and ate with them. This parable deals with a social outcast and shows the Father's love for him.

A. The Younger Son. Lost.

B. The Man (Father). God.

C. The Elder Son. (Pharisees). The Self-Righteous

I. The **Younger** Son.
Anyone who has settled an estate knows there are often misunderstandings and sometimes greed. Instead of waiting for his father to die, this young man sought to take his inheritance now. He "gathered all together", which means he turned them into cash and took his journey.

A. His **Attitude**. (v.12).
He demanded his inheritance, *"Father, give me the portion of goods that falleth unto me."*
He had only one desire and that was to get his hands on the money.

> *"An inheritance may be gotten hastily at the beginning, But the end thereof shall not be blessed".* (Proverbs 20:21)

B. His **Behavior**. (v.13).
He enjoyed *"the pleasures of sin for a season."* (Hebrews 11:25)

Sin is enjoyable for a season, and then the grief, pain, and suffering comes. Soon his money was gone, and so were all his friends.

C. His **Consequences.** (v.14)

An unexpected event took place, a great famine. In desperation, he found himself:

1. **Alone**.

   No one was with him.

2. **Feeding pigs**.

   Debasement. No self-respecting religious Jew would have anything to do with swine.

3. **Starving**.

   Hungry to the point of eating pig slop.

4. **Living** in squalor.

   Having absolutely nothing.

   "Sin will take you further than you wanted to go, keep you longer than you wanted to stay, and cost you more than you wanted to pay."

D. His **awakening.** (vv.17-19)

1. He came to **his senses**. (v.17)

   No one can be helped until they realize they need help.

2. He acknowledged **his sin**. (v.18)

   > *"I came not to call the righteous, but sinners to repentance."* (Luke 5:32)

   Without inward repentance from sin, we only are like "*whited sepulchers, which indeed appear beautiful outward, but are within full of dead men's bones, and of all uncleanness.*" (Matthew 23:27)

3. He was willing to humble himself and become a **servant**. (v.19).

   He knew he was unworthy of any kindness.

His pride was broken.

> *"Pride goeth before destruction, and an haughty spirit before a fall."* (Proverbs 16:18)

II. The **Father**. (vv.20-24)
This man is a representation of God the Father's love for you.

A. He was **waiting** and **watching**.
God does that for you as well.

> *"Have I any pleasure at all that the wicked should die? Saith the Lord God, and not that he should return from his ways, and live?"* (Ezekiel 18:23)

B. He showed **concern** and **compassion**. (vv.20-22)

1. He **ran** to his son and loved him. (v.20)
2. He **accepted** his son's repentance and **forgave** him. (vv.21-22) He was given things a slave would not normally have:

   a. A robe. representing wealth.
   b. A ring. representing restoration, salvation, and authority.
   c. Shoes. representing acceptance. Only a free man and members of the household wore shoes. Not a slave, who would be barefoot.

3. He acknowledged his return with a **celebration**. (v.23).
   What a picture of Christ's love for us.

   > "*All that the Father giveth me shall come to me; and him that cometh to me I will in no wise cast out.*"
   > (John 6:37)

III. The **Elder** Son. (vv.25-32)

A. He was **angry** and **resentful.** v.25-28
   The elder son had done everything that he should have done, and thought that his brother was being rewarded for disobedience.

B. He was **self-righteous.** (vv.25-29)
   He thought he was a better son. Instead he was a bitter son. God is greater than our sin and delights to show mercy (unmerited forgiveness) and grace (unmerited favor). Don't let God's blessing on others blind you to God's desire to restore.

C. He was **unloving.** (vv.30-32)
   Nothing the elder son said was untrue. The elder son is the picture of the Pharisees and Scribes. They did much right, but they missed salvation because they thought they deserved it. The father confirmed his inheritance yet rejoiced to see his younger son.

   > "*beloved if God so loved us, we ought also to love one another.*" (I John 4:11)

IV. What we can Learn from this parable?

    A. God's love for us never ceases.

> "*But God commendeth His love toward us, in that, while we were yet sinners, Christ died for us.*" (Romans 5:8)

    B. God wants us saved.

> "*All that the Father giveth me, shall come to me; and him that cometh to me I will in no wise cast out.*" (John 6:37)

    C. Salvation only comes when we come to ourselves.

> "*And when he came to himself, he said, How many hired servants of my father's have bread enough and to spare, and I perish with hunger?*" (Luke 15:17)

    D. God loves you more in a moment than anyone else could love you in a lifetime.

An Observation:

The prodigal son willfully chose to be lost and willfully chose to be saved.

Lessons 3-2, 3-3, and 3-4
Application

1. Why are people important to God?

2. Are you important to God?

   How do you know this?

3. What are you doing to win others to the Lord?

4. How can you become more active in winning souls?

5. Why is there rejoicing in heaven over one who becomes saved? (Matthew 18:14)

CHAPTER FOUR

PARABLES OF PRAYER

Lesson 4-1   Friend at Midnight   Luke 11:5-1

Lesson 4-2   Persistent Widow and   Luke 18:1-8
              Unjust Judge

Lesson 4-3   Pharisee and the Publican   Luke 18:9-14

Lesson 4-1

Parable of the Friend at Midnight

Luke 11:5-10

Luke 11:5-10

5 *And he said unto them, which of you shall have a friend, and shall go unto him at midnight, and say unto him, Friend, lend me three loaves;*

6 *For a friend of mine in his journey is come to me, and I have nothing to set before him?*

7 *And he from within shall answer and say, Trouble me not: the door is now shut, and my children are with me in bed; I cannot rise and give thee.*

8 *I say unto you, Though he will not rise and give him, because he is his friend, yet because of his importunity he will rise and give him as many as he needs.*

9 *And I say to you, Ask, and it shall be given you; Seek, and you shall find, knock, and it shall be opened to you.*

10 *For everyone that asks receives; and he that seeks finds; And to him that knocks it shall be opened.*

Lesson 4-1

I. The Setting.
   After giving the Lord's Prayer (vv.2-4) as a pattern for effective prayer, Jesus taught about the importance

of persistent prayer. It is not enough to pray and forget. We need to pray and persist.

> *"Pray without ceasing."* (I Thessalonians 5:17). But unlike religions, that chant meaningless words over and over again. Real prayer is designed to express real needs.

After a request to learn how to pray, the Lord Jesus emphasized prayer to the Father, as an important part of his life.

> *"And it came to pass in those days, that He went out into a mountain to pray, and continued all night in prayer to God."* (Luke 6:12)

II. The Story. "A friend comes in his journey."
In order to drive home the importance of persistent prayer, Jesus gives us the story of the arrival of a guest at a sleeping neighbor's home.

A. The **Community**.
In the Middle East, when a guest arrived, the whole village was responsible for entertaining him. To fail to provide for a guest would bring great shame to the house that guest came to, and to the entire village. The Jews listening to Jesus' story would have been embarrassed by the lack of hospitality. Saying "Trouble me not", would be a serious violation of the social code.

B. The **Home**.
Try to what the average home looked like. It was one room with one small window. The room was divided into two parts. Two-thirds of it was on

ground floor, and one-third was slightly raised. On the raised part, the fire burned all night. Families were large and they would sleep on mats, close together for warmth. It was often customary to bring livestock: chickens and goats, into the house. Now you can visualize how crowded the room was.

Then a knock at the door. You have to step over your family and move the animals out of the way to answer the door.

III. A Need **Expressed**. (v.5-6)

Prayer cannot be answered if not prayed.

A. An **Unexpected** Need: after hours.
Three loaves of bread (physical needs). Bread was usually made fresh daily. It went bad quickly. It gives us a better understanding of "Give us this day our daily bread". (v.3)

B. An **Inconvenient** hour: midnight.
Midnight. Most of our problems come at an inconvenient hour, such as breaking a shoelace or running out of gas. Life is made up of surprises.

IV. A Need **Denied.** v.7.

A. Too late. "**Trouble me not**."
Ever notice how no one wants your troubles? If a good friend will help when inconvenienced, how much more will God answer our needs.

B. Too inconvenient. "**I cannot rise**".
Others do not like to be inconvenienced. Rather, "I will not rise". Yet, the obligation of friendship will not be denied.

> *"For we have not an high priest which cannot be touched with the feeling of our infirmities, but was in all points tempted like as we are, yet without sin. Let us therefore come boldly unto the throne of grace, that we may obtain mercy, and find grace to help in time of need".* (Hebrews 4:15-16)

Through Christ we have access to the Father about our needs, desires, and fears.

V. A Need **Fulfilled**. (vv.8-10)

A. **Persistence** pays. God honors commitment to prayer.
Keep praying for your needs, lost loved ones, family, and friends. Once a man dreamed he was hammering on a rock, yet nothing seemed to happen. Full of dust and sweat, he was discouraged and was ready to give up. He complained to God and expressed his frustration. God told him to try again. This time the rock shattered into many pieces.

B. Duty **Triumphs** over inconvenience.
People often do their duty even when inconvenienced. God has a duty toward you. When you become God's child, you become his property.

> "Importunate prayer never faints or grows weary; it is never discouraging; it never yields to cowardice, but is buoyed up and sustained by a hope that knows no despair, and faith which will not let go."
>
> - E. M. Bounds

VI. A Lesson in **How to Pray.** (vv.9-10)

A. **Ask.**
The word used here means continually. We need to ask God. God can't answer non-existent prayer.

B. **Seek.**

1. We need to look for **God's answer**.
2. God expects us to do what **we can**. This man went to his neighbor.

C. **Knock.**
Keep knocking until God answers. We need to persist.

> *"Call unto me, and I will answer thee, and shew thee great and mighty things, which thou knowest not."* (Jeremiah 33:3)

VII. An **Assurance** of God. (vv.11-13)

A. We have a **secure** relationship based on love. (vv.11-12)

B. God specializes in giving **good things**. (v.13). Don't be afraid to pray. God doesn't drop pianos on people's heads. God loves you too much to harm you and is too wise to make a mistake.

C. If we, being evil, give **good gifts** to our children, how much more will God give us **good gifts**?

Don't ever be afraid to pray to God. He knows you and loves you. He has good things for you. Just keep asking and don't give up.

Lesson 4-1
Application

1. Do you pray?

2. Do you have a regular personal prayer time?

3. Do you expect God to answer?

4. Why should you pray?

Lesson 4-2

The Parable of the Persistent Widow and Unjust Judge

Luke 18:1-8

Luke 18:1-8

¹ And he spoke a parable to them to this end, that men ought always to pray, and not to faint;

² Saying, There was in a city a judge, which feared not God, neither regarded man:

³ And there was a widow in that city; and she came unto him, saying, Avenge me of mine adversary.

⁴ And he would not for a while: but afterward he said within himself, Though I fear not God, nor regard man;

⁵ Yet because this widow troubles me, I will avenge her, lest by her continual coming she weary me.

⁶ And the Lord said, Hear what the unjust judge saith.

⁷ And shall not God avenge his own elect, which cry day and night to him, though he bear long with them?

⁸ I tell you that he will avenge them speedily. Nevertheless, when the Son of man comes, shall he find faith on the earth?

Lesson 4-2

In order to encourage prayer, Jesus gave the parable about an unjust judge. In Jesus' day, there was no city courthouse, and a judge would travel from town to town, staying for a few days at a time. If his docket was filled, a bribe to an assistant could help him get his case heard.

> "And thou shalt take no gift; for the gift blindeth the wise, and perverteth the words of the righteous." (Exodus 23:8)

> "A wicked man taketh a gift out of the bosom to pervert the ways of judgment." (Proverbs 17:23)

I. The Widow's **Plight**.

   A. A widow said, "Avenge me of mine adversary." (Luke 18:3)
This poor widow had very **few resources** at her disposal. She could not bribe the judge to get an audience, even if she wanted to. Perhaps she was totally ignored.

   B. Widows in our Lord's day were **despised** and preyed upon by unprincipled men. They had no one to protect them and their only hope for justice was through the law.

   C. Women were **second-class** citizens at best. Women were often taken for granted and rarely could rise in power and position.

   D. She had **no husband** to stand with her.

   E. Being a **widow** she could not afford legal representation.

   F. Her only recourse was to be **persistent** in pleading to the judge.

II. The **Unjust** Judge. (vv.2,4-5)
This judge had **no regard** for anyone but himself.
This widow could do nothing for him.

A. The judge cared **nothing** about the widow's plight. (v.2,4)

1. **Religious obligation** did not cause him to act. (v.2,4)
Without fear of God, there is no respect of man.

2. **Social justice** did not move him to act. (v.2,4)
Without respect for man, there is only apathy toward their plight.

B. The judge only cared about his own **convenience**. (v.5)
He was tired of hearing her petition for justice. The widow's persistence resulted in her request being granted by the judge, *"lest by her continual coming she weary me."*

C. He feared no one, not God or man.

D. Her persistence wore him out.

E. He judged not because it was right but because it was the easy thing to do.

> *"Ye shall not afflict any widow, or fatherless child. If thou afflict them in any wise, and they cry at all unto me, I will surely hear their cry."* (Exodus 22:22-23)

> *"Pure religion and undefiled before God and the Father is this: to visit the fatherless and widows in their*

affliction, and to keep oneself unspotted from the world." (James 1:27)

III. A look at the **Lord**. (v.6-8)
Jesus gave this parable to teach us what our attitudes should be toward prayer.

A. God is willing to **hear** and answer our prayer. (v.7)
We appear before God not as outsiders, but as his children.

B. God **answers** our prayer on his schedule. (v.7)

C. God will speedily **avenge** his own elect. (v.8)

> *"Vengeance is mine; I will repay, saith the Lord."* (Romans 12:19)

Remember, God cares for his children. If an unjust judge will eventually respond, how much more will the Just Judge respond to our pleas?

IV. Lessons to be learned.

> *"When the Son of man cometh, shall He find faith on earth?"* (v.8)

Will Christ find people praying when he returns?

What about now?

Do you pray to God? Consider these reasons why people fail to pray:

A. Prayer becomes a **burden** instead of a **blessing**. It becomes a ritual or a program. Prayer is an amazing opportunity to come unto the presence of God.

B. Prayer is not answered according to our **expectations**.
This attitude expects God to do what we want rather, that what he desires. Luke 22:42 gives us Christ's words before His arrest and crucifixion.

> *"Father, if thou be willing, remove this cup from me: nevertheless not my will, but thine, be done."*

C. Prayer seems as if God gives no answer. But God does answer three ways:

1. **YES**.
   He does this immediately, or over time.
2. **NO**.
   He does this because it is not good for us.
3. **WAIT**.
   He does this because the time isn't right.

V. Other thoughts on our prayer life.
George Müller (1805-1898), a pastor and orphanage director, was known for his faith and persistent prayer. When he prayed for the specific needs for his orphanage, God sent exactly what was required. Yet, for more than forty years, he also prayed for the conversion of a friend, and his friend's son. When Müller died, these men were still unconverted. God answered those prayers however, in his own time. The friend was converted while attending Müller's funeral, and his son was converted a week later!

A. We need to **be sincere** in our prayers.

B. We are to **be persistent** in prayer.

> *"But seek ye first the kingdom of God, and His righteousness; and all these things shall be added unto you."* (Matthew 6:33)

C. Faith is a rare commodity.
   Faith is more than just believing God will hear our prayer. In this instance, it goes beyond that to encompass the whole body of faith once delivered to the saints. (Jude v.3)

D. Don't give up praying. Have a special burden or need? Keep praying.

Set a regular time to pray to God.

Lesson 4-2
Application

1. Does God hear everyone's prayer?

2. Will God respond to your prayer?

3. Will prayer exempt us from trials?

4. Can we depend on God to be just?

5. What should we be praying for?

Lesson 4-3

The Parable of the Pharisee and the Publican

Luke 18:9-14

Luke 18:9-14

⁹ *And he spoke this parable to certain which trusted in themselves that they were righteous, and despised others:*

¹⁰ *Two men went up into the temple to pray; the one a Pharisee, and the other a publican.*

¹¹ *The Pharisee stood and prayed thus with himself, God, I thank thee, that I am not as other men are, extortioners, unjust, adulterers, or even as this publican.*

¹² *I fast twice in the week, I give tithes of all that I possess.*

¹³ *And the publican, standing afar off, would not lift up so much as his eyes unto heaven, but smote upon his breast, saying, God be merciful to me a sinner.*

¹⁴ *I tell you, this man went down to his house justified rather than the other: for every one that exalts himself shall be abased; and he that humbles himself shall be exalted.*

Lesson 4-3

After teaching about persistent prayer, Luke 18:1-8, Jesus teaches on acceptable prayer. To do this, Jesus tells us this parable, "*Two men went up into the temple*

to pray; the one a Pharisee, and the other a publican."
(v.10)

I. The **Pharisee**.

A. The name Pharisee comes from the Hebrew word *"perushim"*, which means *"separated"*. The origin of the Pharisees began during the era of the Second Temple (536 B.C. −70 A.D.) in the time of Ezra. The Pharisees emphasized the oral reading of the law, especially the first five books of the Bible. They were considered experts and accurate expositors of Jewish law. The Pharisees also were in charge of local synagogues and held literal interpretation of God's Word. Outward appearance became a means by which to proclaim their spiritual commitment, and set themselves apart from others.

B. His **Pride**. (vv.11-12)

1. His **Appearance.** A properly dressed Pharisee would have flowing robes and a prayer shawl.

   "And when thou prayest, thou shalt not be as the hypocrites are; for they love to pray standing in the synagogues and in the corners of the streets, that they be seen of men. Verily I say unto you, they have their reward." (Matthew 6:5)

2. His **Attitude.** He **despised** others.

   a. The word 'despised' used here literally means "to count as nothing". He lacked compassion, and had no respect for others who were different. There was no sense of humility or need of repentance.

b. Self-righteous and **proud**. He stood apart from others who were inferior. Note his prayer where he thanked God that *"I am not as other men are."* (v.11)

> *"Every one that is proud in heart is an abomination to the Lord; though hand join in hand, he shall not be unpunished."* (Proverbs 16:5)

c. He accomplished **nothing**. He asked for nothing, confessed nothing, and received nothing.

3. His **Acceptance.** As a Pharisee, he would be highly respected among the "common people", as one who had obtained spiritual maturity. He would be expected to know what God's mind was concerning doctrine and life in general.

4. His **Accomplishment.** His apparent spiritual life was one to be admired. Note what he had accomplished:

a. Different from others. (v.11)
b. Fast twice a week. (v.12)
c. Tither. (v.12)

These acts of worship were beyond what the law required, as set forth in the book of Leviticus. Such things are important, but without repentance, they are worthless!

> "*For I bear them record that they have a zeal of God, but not according to knowledge. For they being ignorant of God's righteousness, and going about to establish their own righteousness, have not submitted themselves unto the righteousness of God.*" (Romans 10:2-3)

II. The **Publican.** (vv.13-14)

A. Publicans were Jews who collaborated with the Romans. They were best known for collecting taxes. They were considered extortionists and traitors, because they served Rome. Assigned to collect a prescribed amount of taxes, anything paid beyond that was theirs to keep. Therefore, they were aggressive in their efforts to extract as much money as they could, from their fellow citizens. They were universally hated by their contemporaries.

  1. His **Appearance.** He stood apart, and was avoided by others, because of his shame. He was rich but he avoided others.
  2. His **Attitude.** His eyes were cast down as he smote his breast, asking God to be merciful. His seven-word prayer touched God's heart. The Pharisee's thirty-four word prayer shut God's heart.
  3. His **Acceptance.** He was more concerned about what God thought, than what people

thought. He sought God's forgiveness. His short prayer contains the three elements of forgiveness: humility, confession, and repentance.

a. **Humility**.

> "Humble yourselves in the sight of the Lord, and he shall lift you up." (James 4:10)

b. **Confession**.

> "If we confess our sins, he is faithful and just to forgive us our sins, and to cleanse us from all unrighteousness." (I John 1:9)

c. **Repentance**.

> "I tell you, Nay; but except ye repent, ye shall all likewise perish." (Luke 13:3)

B. His **Achievement.**

The word justification means "to be declared right" before God. He was justified before God.

> "And ye shall seek me, and find me, when ye shall search for me with all your heart." (Jeremiah 29:13)

III. A **Comparison** of the Pharisee and the Publican. These two individuals were socially apart in their appearance, attitude, acceptance, and achievement. One was forgiven by God, and one was rejected.

"Repent ye therefore, and be converted, that your sins may be blotted out, when the times of refreshing shall come from the presence of the Lord." (Acts 3:19)

IV. Some **Observations** about Pride.

  A. Pride talks about itself.

  B. Pride seldom admits a need.

  C. Pride sees fault with others.

  D. Pride stresses performance rather than inward purity.

Lesson 4-3
Application

1. Do you think you are spiritually better than others?

2. Are you proud of your goodness?

3. Do you make other people feel welcome at church?

4. Do you reach out to others, especially the social outcasts?

5. Do you worship God from your heart or from your tradition?

   How do you know?

6. Do you acknowledge that you are a sinner saved by God's grace?

CHAPTER FIVE

PARABLES OF FORGIVENESS

Lesson 5-1   Unmerciful Servant   Matt 18:21-35

Lesson 5-2   Two Debtors   Luke 7:41-43

Lesson 5-1

Parable of The Unmerciful Servant

Matthew 18:21-35

Matthew 18:21-35

²¹ Then came Peter to him, and said, Lord, how oft shall my brother sin against me, and I forgive him? till seven times?

²² Jesus saith unto him, I say not unto thee, Until seven times: but, until seventy times seven.

²³ Therefore is the kingdom of heaven likened unto a certain king, which would take account of his servants.

²⁴ And when he had begun to reckon, one was brought unto him, which owed him ten thousand talents.

²⁵ But forasmuch as he had not to pay, his lord commanded him to be sold, and his wife, and children, and all that he had, and payment to be made.

²⁶ The servant therefore fell down, and worshipped him, saying, Lord, have patience with me, and I will pay thee all.

²⁷ Then the lord of that servant was moved with compassion, and loosed him, and forgave him the debt.

²⁸ But the same servant went out, and found one of his fellow servants, which owed him an hundred pence: and he laid hands on him, and took him by the throat, saying, pay me that thou owes.

²⁹ *And his fellow servant fell down at his feet, and besought him, saying, Have patience with me, and I will pay thee all.*

³⁰ *And he would not: but went and cast him into prison, till he should pay the debt.*

³¹ *So when his fellow servants saw what was done, they were very sorry, and came and told unto their lord all that was done.*

³² *Then his lord, after that he had called him, said unto him, O thou wicked servant, I forgave thee all that debt, because thou desired me:*

³³ *Should not thou also have had compassion on thy fellow servant, even as I had pity on thee?*

³⁴ *And his lord was wroth, and delivered him to the tormentors, till he should pay all that was due unto him.*

³⁵ *So likewise shall my heavenly Father do also unto you, if ye from your hearts forgive not every one his brother their trespasses.*

Lesson 5-1

When Peter came to Jesus, he asked an important question regarding forgiveness. The rabbis of Jesus' day taught that forgiving someone three times was sufficient. Peter suggested seven times, which would appear generous. Jesus' reply of *"seventy times seven"* (v.22), must have come as a shock to Peter. The idea expressed here is not 490 times, but unlimited forgiveness. It is a picture of God's unlimited forgiveness of our sins.

I. The Story.

> *"A certain king, which would take account of his **servants**."* (v.2)

This parable is a teaching on the Kingdom of Heaven, which represents all who claim to be saved.

A. The King represents **God**.
Only God has limitless resources.

B. The servants represents **believers**.
Each believer owes different amounts of sin.

C. Debt represents **sin**.
This sin debt is absolutely unpayable.

II. Observations about **Forgiveness**.

A. Forgiveness is not a question of how many transgressions, but rather how much **grace**.

> *"And forgive us our debts, as we forgive our debtors."* (Matthew 6:12)

You are expected to forgive others. The level of forgiveness we give others affects the forgiveness God gives us in this life. This is not a story dealing with salvation.

B. When God forgives, He forgives our massive **debt**.

> *"He has not dealt with us after our sins; nor rewarded us according to our iniquities."* (Psalm 103:10)

> *"Like as a father pitied his children, so the LORD pitied them that fear Him."* (Psalm 103:12)

Ten thousand talents is a massive sum. One talent is equivalent to twenty years of labor. The amount owed is staggering as it would be impossible for the average person, let alone a king to repay. In 2 Chronicles 25:6, Amaziah, king of the southern kingdom of Judah, hired *"an hundred thousand soldiers"*, for one *"hundred talents of silver"*, out of the northern kingdom of Israel.

C. God is incredibly **compassionate**. (vv.25-27)
It was the common practice, in accordance with ancient customs, to exact payment, by selling a person's assets and freedom if they were unable to pay their debt. Instead, this king forgave all the debt.

D. Our **unwillingness** to forgive, (vv.28-35)
When we are unwilling to forgive, it causes God to hold back his blessings and forgive our trespasses against Him. This forgiven servant quickly forgot the mercy shown him. The hundred pence owed him by a fellow servant was worth the equivalent of a few dollars, perhaps less than fifteen.

> *"Forgiving...even as God for Christ's sake hath forgiven you."* (Ephesians 4:32)

III. **Levels** of Forgiveness.

A. Hurt committed through **ignorance** or **immaturity**. Usually this involves a child or someone not understanding or knowing what they are doing.

B. Hurt committed yet **sincerely** apologized for by the offender. We are to forgive immediately without regret or haste.

C. Hurt **half** apologized for, where the offender apologizes yet accuses us of wrong behavior, which caused their wrong behavior. Usually words such as *"I was wrong, but you did this!"* are spoken.

D. Hurt done **intentionally** or **maliciously** with no apology given. You forgive, not because the person deserves to be forgiven, but because you deserve to be emotionally free from stress.

Perhaps there is someone who has hurt you. You have held bitterness and pain within your heart and mind. Let it go! Forgive not because they deserve it, but rather because you have been forgiven by God, in spite of your sin against him. Don't allow someone to live "rent free" in your mind to torment you. Live at a higher level, and forgive those who need your forgiveness. You will have a happier, better life for it.

Lesson 5-1
Application

1. Why must we forgive these who trespass against us?

2. What happens to our relationship with God if we harbor bitterness, anger, or a lack of compassion?

3. Have you forgiven those who have sinned against you?

Lesson 5-2

Parable of the Two Debtors

Luke 7:41-43

Luke 7:41-43

41 There was a certain creditor which had two debtors: the one owed five hundred pence, and the other fifty.

42 And when they had nothing to pay, he frankly forgave them both. Tell me therefore, which of them will love him most?

43 Simon answered and said, I suppose that he, to whom he forgave most. And he said unto him, Thou hast rightly judged.

Lesson 5-2

A Pharisee named Simon, invited Jesus and others to his home for a meal, (v.36). However, Jesus was not treated graciously or with respect. A host would normally greet and welcome the arrival of a guest to his home, with the washing the guest's feet to remove the road dirt, giving a welcoming kiss, and anointing his head with oil. Jesus did not receive this traditional respect of a fellow rabbi.

During the meal, an uninvited woman of poor repute arrived and worshiped the Lord at his feet, with tears, and great respect and honor. (v.38). Simon was offended at her presence and actions, and reasoned in his mind. Jesus then shared a parable about two debtors.

I. The Story. A certain creditor which had two debtors.

   A. **Debtors.** Sinners.

      1. The first debtor owed five hundred denarii, about two years of wages.

      2. The second debtor owed one-tenth that amount, or about fifty denarii, or about two and a half months of wages.

   B. **Debt.** Sin.
Something owed that cannot be repaid.

> *"For all have sinned, and come short of the glory of God".* (Romans 3:23)

   C. **Pharisee.** Self-Righteous.
A religious leader, who was worshipping at the temple, Pharisees were responsible for serving and leading the worship and religious functions at a local synagogue. He strictly kept and defended the Judaic laws and traditions. He was self-righteous, believing he was a holy man.

   D. **Creditor,** or Money Lender. Jesus Christ (God).
The one who loans money (with interest) to others who are in need, with a contract to receive the payment back for monies loaned out. If the loan is defaulted, the creditor would have the right to seize any or all properties and assets the borrower had, to pay off the debt.

II. Jesus tells a parable. (vv.41-43)

   A. Two debtors are unable to pay off their debt. One owes five hundred denarii (about two years wage), the other fifty denarii (about two and a half month's wages).

B. And remarkably, the creditor forgives both their debts, no strings attached.

C. Jesus asks simply, Which debtor would be more grateful?

III. The Interpretation.

A. The response of the Pharisee reflected his own hard-hearted attitude, and a lack of compassion towards others.

B. The one who is forgiven much, loves those who forgive more. It is not unusual to see someone greatly overcome by sin have a completely radical change in their attitude and dedication to God.

IV. Lessons to be **learned**.

A. The one needing the most forgiving loves the **most**. This "sinner" knows he deserves judgment.

B. The one needing forgiving here is **you**.
We don't see the depravity of our own hearts.

C. Each one of us owes a **debt** to God which we cannot pay.

> *"For all have sinned, and come short of the glory of God."* (Romans 3:23)

D. Our ministry is one of **restoration**, not condemnation.
Like Jesus, we should desire to restore a person. We must not judge a fallen person, but rather seek to restore them to a relationship with God.

> *"If a man be overtaken in a fault, ye which are spiritual, restore such*

an one in the spirit of meekness; considering thyself, lest thou also be tempted." (Galatians 6:1)

Another useful verse,

"A new commandment I give unto you, that ye love one another; as I have loved you, that ye also love one another."
(John 13:34)

Do you have a heart that sees other people hurting?

When a brother or sister has stumbled into sin, do you have a spirit of compassion?

or, are you self-righteous like the Pharisee?

Are you like Jesus, "a friend of sinners?"

Lesson 5-2
Application

1. Why is it so easy to see the sins of others?

2. Why is it so hard to see our own sins?

3. If someone has sinned against us, how should we deal with it?

4. What are you doing to address the sin you have committed against others?

CHAPTER SIX

Parables of How to Live Our Lives

Lesson 6-1   House on the Rock   Matt 7:24-27
             (Two Foundations)
                                    Luke 6:46-49

Lesson 6-2   Good Samaritan   Luke 10:30-37

Lesson 6-3   The Good Shepherd   John 10:1-18

Lesson 6-1

Parable of the House on the Rock

Matthew 7:24-27; Luke 6:46-49

Matthew 7:24-27

24 Therefore whosoever hear these sayings of mine, and does them, I will liken him unto a wise man, which built his house upon a rock:

25 And the rain descended, and the floods came, and the winds blew, and beat upon that house; and it fell not: for it was founded upon a rock.

26 And every one that heareth these sayings of mine, and does them not, shall be likened unto a foolish man, which built his house upon the sand:

27 And the rain descended, and the floods came, and the winds blew, and beat upon that house; and it fell: and great was the fall of it.

Lesson 6-1

In 1174 A.D., Italian architect Bonanno Pisano (1150-1200) began his most famous work, a bell tower for the Cathedral of the city of Pisa. The eight story, 185-foot tall structure had one major problem. The ground was too soft. If fact, the word Pisa means "marsh land". A ten-foot deep foundation was totally inadequate. The tower continued to shift until it was seventeen feet out of plumb. More than $30 million dollars has been spent to restore the lean it had two centuries earlier. 110 tons of dirt have been removed and the foundation was reinforced with concrete. The Tower of Pisa has a weak foundation. Eventually, it will fall over!

Jesus spoke about the foundation in our lives. This parable was at the conclusion of the Sermon on The Mount (Matthew chapters 5-7), and it addresses our salvation and commitment to live for God.

I. The Setting.

  A. After the conclusion of Christ's Sermon on the Mount, this parable was given.

  B. The emphasis is on the genuineness of our relationship to God.

II. The Story.

  "*Therefore, whosoever heareth these sayings of mine, and doeth them*". (v.24)

  A. The Symbols on **Obedience**.
  The Lord dealt the issue of obedience. What is important is what is taking place on the inside. Everyone of us is building a life. How we build affects our eternity.

  B. The **symbols** of this parable:

  1. Rock represents **Christ**.
  2. House represents **our lives.**
  3. Rain, Floods, and Wind represent **testing** and **judgment**.
  4. Sand represents a **false foundation**.

III.   The way we **build** our lives.

A. *"For other foundation can no man lay than that is laid, which is Jesus Christ. Now if any man build upon this foundation gold, silver, precious stones, wood, hay stubble; Every man's work shall be made manifest: for the day shall declare it, because it shall be revealed by fire; and the fire shall try every man's work of what sort it is. If any man's work abides which he hath built thereupon, he shall receive a reward. If any man's work shall be burned, he shall suffer loss: but he himself shall be saved; yet so as by fire."* (1 Corinthians 3:11-15)

1. **What** did we build **on?** (v.11)
   That foundation for the Christian is Jesus Christ. He is our salvation.
2. **What** did we build? (vv.12-14)
   Our works for Christ will be judged for reward. Did you do anything for God?
3. **Why** did we build? (vv.14-15)
   Did we build for Christ's glory or our own?
4. **How** did we build? (v.15).
   What methods did we use? God's or the world's ?

IV. The **similarity** and **difference** between each builder. There are two types of people in the world: wise and foolish.

A. The **similarity**.
   What they have in common:

1. They both **heard** God's Word. (vv. 24, 26)
2. They both **built**, (vv. 24-26)
3. They both experienced a **storm**. (vv. 25, 27)

B. The **difference**.

1. The wise builder heard and obeyed, (a picture of **obedience**). What he built withstood the storm, (a picture of **salvation**).
The foolish builder heard and ignored, (a Picture of **disobedience**).

   > *"But be ye doers of the word, and not hearers only, deceiving your own selves."* (James 1:22)

2. The wise **survived** the rain, flood and winds, (a picture of trials and judgment) without losing his house.
The **foolish lost all**. He had built on sand (a picture of **self will**) and his house fell in ruin (a picture of **total judgment**) and he lost all.

Every one of us is building a life.

Have you trusted Jesus as your foundation?

Are you saved?

Beyond that, are you building anything of spiritual value for eternity? When you stand before God, will you have anything to show?

Are you serving God?

Make sure you are building a life for God that matters for eternity.

Lesson 6-1
Application

1. What are you building your life on?

2. Can you escape life's storms?

3. What is the spiritual application of this parable?

4. Why would anyone build on a different foundation?

5. What is the benefit from building a life on Christ?

LESSON 6-2

PARABLE OF THE GOOD SAMARITAN

Luke 10:30-37

Luke 10:30-37

³⁰ *And Jesus answering said, A certain man went down from Jerusalem to Jericho, and fell among thieves, which stripped him of his raiment, and wounded him, and departed, leaving him half dead.*

³¹ *And by chance there came down a certain priest that way: and when he saw him, he passed by on the other side.*

³² *And likewise a Levite, when he was at the place, came and looked on him, and passed by on the other side.*

³³ *But a certain Samaritan, as he journeyed, came where he was: and when he saw him, he had compassion on him,*

³⁴ *And went to him, and bound up his wounds, pouring in oil and wine, and set him on his own beast, and brought him to an inn, and took care of him.*

³⁵ *And on the morrow when he departed, he took out two pence, and gave them to the host, and said unto him, Take care of him; and whatsoever thou spends more, when I come again, I will repay thee.*

³⁶ *Which now of these three, thinks you, was neighbor unto him that fell among the thieves?*

³⁷ *And he said, He that showed mercy on him. Then said Jesus unto him, Go, and do thou likewise.*

Lesson 6-2

I. The Story: *"A certain man went down from Jerusalem to Jericho."* (v.30)
    The road from Jerusalem to Jericho was dangerous journey of fifteen miles. Since temple workers travel is so much, one would think that the road would be secure, but such was not the case.

II. Let's look at the five people involved in this story of the Good Samaritan.

    A. The **victim.** (v.30) Unknown origin.

        1. Identity and heritage.
        2. No known sin or crimes.
        3. Was just "passing through."

    B. The **Thieves.** (v.30) Seeking a victim to exploit.

        1. They stripped the victim of his raiment (clothes and possessions).
        2. They beat him and left him "half dead".
        3. They departed without any care or concern.

    C. The **Priest.** (v.31) A man of scripture and highly regarded in his sect.

        1. He walked by without stopping or looking. Was he in a hurry?
        2. He avoided the victim by not stopping, but continuing to walk on the other side of the road.
        3. He was too busy "serving God", and did not want to defile himself.

D. The **Levite.** (v.32) A man (lawyer) who defended the religious law.

1. He apparently did not know him and did not want to get involved.
2. He stopped or slowed down to get a look.
3. He passed on the other side of the road. The victim was a 'nuisance' to be avoided.

E. The **Samaritan.** (vv.33-35) The victim was a person he could help.

1. He **looked** on the need of the victim and had compassion.
2. He **rearranged** his schedule to accommodate him. There was no logical reason why he should. Giving "mercy" doesn't need a reason.
3. He spent his own money to **comfort** him. "Oil, wine, the inn", and "two pence" (two days of wages for a laborer)."
4. He did so **without thought**, not seeking any reward. No one ever told him how wonderful he was. He never received a penny back. He did it because it was the right thing to do.

III. History.

The Samaritan was a man from a totally different culture, which had, with a history of animosity between the Jews and Samaritans. In 721 B.C., the Northern Kingdom fell to the Assyrians, and had deported most of the Jewish population and resettled pagans from their other conquered lands. The Jews who remained, intermarried, and compromised God's Word by assimilating pagan practices. This development led to a breakdown of the relationship with religious Jews of the Southern Kingdom. The

Jews excluded the Samaritans and showed hatred toward them. The Samaritans returned the same feelings.

IV. Look at Opportunities.
Which of these three men (priest, Levite, or Samaritan) was a neighbor? Jesus summed it up in verses 36-37. The answer is wherever there is a need, we need to be a neighbor.

A. Jesus wants us to deal with **concrete** needs rather than talking about **abstract** ideals. Anyone can talk about world hunger, or homelessness. It is another thing to do something about it.

B. Jesus wants to move us from **duty** to **devotion** (to him), from **debating** to **doing**. We need to help others.

V. Some Observations

A. The high cost of caring is not as expensive as the cost of not caring.
When you see others in need and harden your heart, we fail to serve God help others. We lose opportunities to become better men and women, and stewards of God's grace.

B. The Levites and priests could have been a good influence for God. Instead they left a bad one that discredited their faith.

C. The Samaritan's one deed of mercy has inspired sacrificial ministry all over the world.

D. What kind of neighbor will you be? I trust it will be one who shows concern for others. On television, we often see relief efforts for others presented by actors and actresses. How much more could be done if those actors and actresses would reach into their own pockets and give sacrificially toward the causes they claim to care so much about?

Lesson 6-2
Application

1. Who was the good neighbor? Why?

2. Are you a good neighbor to the unlovable?

3. Who are you reaching out to help?

4. How can you be a good neighbor to others?

5. When do you plan to start reaching out as a good neighbor?

Lesson 6-3

Parable of the Good Shepherd

John 10:1-18

John 10:1-18

1 Verily, verily, I say unto you, He that enters not by the door into the sheepfold, but climb up some other way, the same is a thief and a robber.

2 But he that enters in by the door is the shepherd of the sheep.

3 To him the porter opens; and the sheep hear his voice: and he calls his own sheep by name, and leads them out.

4 And when he puts forth his own sheep, he goes before them, and the sheep follow him: for they know his voice.

5 And a stranger will they not follow, but will flee from him: for they know not the voice of strangers.

6 This parable spoke Jesus unto them: but they understood not what things they were which he spoke unto them.

7 Then said Jesus unto them again, Verily, verily, I say unto you, I am the door of the sheep.

8 All that ever came before me are thieves and robbers: but the sheep did not hear them.

9 I am the door: by me if any man enters in, he shall be saved, and shall go in and out, and find pasture.

10 The thief comes not, but for to steal, and to kill, and to destroy: I am come that they might have life, and that they might have it more abundantly.

11 *I am the good shepherd: the good shepherd gives his life for the sheep.*

12 *But he that is an hireling, and not the shepherd, whose own the sheep are not, sees the wolf coming, and leaves the sheep, and flees: and the wolf catches them, and scatters the sheep.*

13 *The hireling flees, because he is an hireling, and cares not for the sheep.*

14 *I am the good shepherd, and know my sheep, and am known of mine.*

15 *As the Father knows me, even so know I the Father: and I lay down my life for the sheep.*

16 *And other sheep I have, which are not of this fold: them also I must bring, and they shall hear my voice; and there shall be one fold, and one shepherd.*

17 *Therefore does my Father love me, because I lay down my life, that I might take it again.*

18 *No man takes it from me, but I lay it down of myself. I have power to lay it down, and I have power to take it again. This commandment have I received of my Father.*

Lesson 6-3

This is the only parable found in the Gospel of John. This "parable" is unique in that the word translated "parable" in verse 6 is better rendered "proverb or figure of speech".

In Jesus' time, a shepherd knew his sheep by name. He would be familiar with each sheep and its particular physical defects, temperament, and tastes. Sometimes this knowledge was reflected in the sheep's name. Shepherding was a hard life with exposure to the elements, long hours, and low pay. It took great sacrifice to be a good shepherd. Dangers were present in the wildlife, including lions, bears, wolves; robbers, weather, and diseases.

It is interesting to note that Christ's miraculous birth was announced first to lowly shepherds, as recorded in Luke 2. Jesus compares believers to sheep. How can you tell if you are one of his sheep?

I. The Setting.

    A. After healing a man born blind. (v.9:1)

    B. After the Pharisees reviled the man born blind. (v.9:28)

    C. After the Pharisees claimed to be Moses' disciple.

II. The Story. "*I am the good Shepherd.*" (v.11)

    A. Door. Christ.

    B. Sheepfold. Assembly of believers, salvation.

    C. Thief/Robber. Unbeliever.

    D. Porter. Christ.

    E. Stranger. False shepherd.

    F. Shepherd. Christ.

    G. Hireling. Convenient shepherd.

    H. Wolf. Devil, danger.

    I. Other Sheep. Gentiles.

III. The Shepherd.
    When a shepherd watered his flock, or entered a field, he had no fear that his sheep would become mixed with other flocks, because when he called,

they would follow him. If a sheep does not follow, that is a sign of illness or injury. Jesus is described as our Shepherd.

A. The **Good** Shepherd. (John 10:10,15)

> *"A righteous man regardeth the life of his beast: but the tender mercies of the wicked are cruel."* (Proverbs 12:10)

B. The **Great** Shepherd.

> *"Now the God of peace, that brought again from the dead our Lord Jesus, that great shepherd of the sheep, through the blood of the everlasting covenant."* (Hebrews 13:20)

C. The **Chief** Shepherd.

> *"For ye were as sheep going astray; but are now returned unto the Shepherd and Bishop of your souls."* (1 Peter 2:25)

IV. The Shepherd **Provides** for his Sheep.

A. His Ministry.

1. By character. *"The Lord is my shepherd; I shall not want."* (Psalm 23:1)
2. By choice . (John 10:15,17)

B. His relationship.

1. He **owns** the sheep. (v.14)

> *"for ye are bought with a price: therefore glorify God in your*

body, and in your spirit, which are God's."
(1 Corinthians 6:20)

2. He **calls** His sheep. (vv.14, 28)
   When he calls his sheep, they will follow.
3. He **leads** the sheep. (Psalm 23:2)

   "He maketh me to lie down in green pastures: he leadeth me beside the still waters."

4. He willingly **gives** his life for the sheep. (vv.11-28)
   Hirelings have no heart for the work and flee when danger comes. Their only concern is financial. They have a job, not a ministry. Their heart is on the world and not the Lord.
5. He **protects** his sheep from danger. (v.8)
   Thieves and robbers were a constant threat. Jesus speaks of being a door. (v.9). The shepherd would sleep in the entryway of a cave or stone enclosure fence. That way, if someone entered or a sheep attempted to leave, they would have to go over the shepherd. *"I am the door."* (v.7)
6. He **willingly dies** for the sheep. (v.17-18)

   "And when Jesus had cried with a loud voice, he said, Father, into thy hands I commend my spirit: and having said thus, he gave up the ghost." (Luke 23:46)

V. Christ as the Door.

  A. He is the way to salvation.

  B. There is no other way.

>   *"Neither is there salvation in any other; for there is none other name under heaven given among men, whereby we must be saved."* (Acts 4:12)

  Are you one of His sheep?

Lesson 6-3
Application

1. Why do people follow hirelings instead of the Shepherd?

2. How can you tell God's voice?

3. How can you tell if your pastor is a shepherd or a hireling?

4. Are there other ways to salvation besides Jesus Christ?

5. What are the dangers Christians face?

CHAPTER SEVEN

Parables of Service and Rewards

Lesson 7-1   Obedient Servant   Luke 17:7-10
              (Unprofitable Servant)

Lesson 7-2   Ten Pounds (Ten Minas)   Luke 19:11-27

Lesson 7-3   Vineyard Laborers   Matt 20:1-16

Lesson 7-4   Talents   Matt 25:14-30

Lesson 7-1

Parable of the Obedient Servant

(Unprofitable Servant)

Luke 17:7-10

Luke 17:7-10

7 But which of you, having a servant plowing or feeding cattle, will say unto him by and by, when he is come from the field, Go and sit down to meat?

8 And will not rather say unto him, Make ready wherewith I may sup, and gird yourself, and serve me, till I have eaten and drunken; and afterward you shalt eat and drink?

9 Does he thank that servant because he did the things that were commanded him? I think not.

10 So likewise ye, when you shall have done all those things which are commanded you, say, We are unprofitable servants: we have done that which was our duty to do.

Lesson 7-1

We live in a world where people feel entitled. They expect free food, shelter, phone, health care, and college education. They believe that they deserve it and will try to take it by force if necessary. This attitude of entitlement has also extended into the church. Some expect the convenience of comfortable pews (with their own special seat), and entertaining programs without any discomfort or commitment.

What happens when we lose our perspective on being servants, and seek to be served? Your focus will shift to your own needs and you will ignore the needs of others. This reveals itself through complaining directly to the church leadership, the messages proclaimed, and other believers. Bible reading, prayer, and attendance become a chore rather than a privilege. The giving, witnessing, and singing suffers as our hearts are not right with God.

In the parable of the Unprofitable Servant, or "slave", Jesus explains our duty and responsibility as Christians to our Lord.

I. Our **Responsibility.** (v.7-9)

A. There is **work** to be done. (v.7)
    In this servant's case, this included feeding the cattle, plowing the field, planting seed, reaping the harvest, cleaning the house, preparing the food, setting the table, and **serving** the master.

B. There was no time to be **idle.** (v.7)
    God expects you to be busy. Note that these tasks were ordinary daily duties and responsibilities.

    > "Behold I say unto you, lift up your eyes, and look on the fields; for they are white already to harvest." (John 4:35)

    Some, however, have given up serving.

    1. Some have **sin** in their lives that **hinders** them from serving.

2. Some have grown **weary** and have taken a permanent **rest**.

3. Some have become **lazy** and seek others to serve them.

C. There is a place to **serve** and a **job** to do. This servant had responsibility and you do too!

> "And he that reapeth receiveth wages, and gathereth fruit unto life eternal: that both he that soweth and he that reapeth may rejoice together. And herein is that saying true, One soweth and another reapeth."
> (John 4:36-37)

No one is exempt from serving God.

D. There is a reasonable expectation of service. (v.7-9). Note three rhetorical questions:

1. "But which of you having a servant plowing or feeding cattle will say unto him by and by, when he is come from the field, 'Go and sit down to meat'?" (v.8)

2. "And will not rather say unto him, 'Make ready wherewith I may sup, and gird thyself and serve me, till I have eaten and drunken, and afterward thou shall eat and drink'?" (v.8)

3. "Doth he thank that servant because he did the things that were commanded him." (v.9)

E. Servants were not expected to be thanked.

II. Our **Attitude**. (v.10)

A. Do you ever feel like God owes you something? God declared Job to be *"perfect and upright, and one that feareth God, and eschewed evil."*(Job 1:1) Yet, in spite of Job's righteousness, he suffered because of it.

B. God is good. He delights in rewarding His servants, not because He has to, but because He wants to.

C. *"Therefore, my beloved brethren, be ye steadfast, unmovable, always abounding in the work of the Lord, forasmuch as ye know that your labor is not in vain in the Lord."*
(1 Corinthians 15:58)

D. John Wesley said,

> "Though we are unprofitable servants to Christ, serving him is not unprofitable to us. For he is pleased to give by his grace a value to our good works, which consequence of His promise entitles us to an eternal reward."

E. We have no claim for reward of obedience.

> *"For by grace are ye saved through faith; and that not of yourselves: it is the gift of God: Not of works, lest any man should boast."*
> (Ephesians 2:8-9)

III. Some **Observations.**

A. The emphasis on this parable is on the quality of **faith**, not quantity.

> *"But without faith it is impossible to please him: for he that cometh to God must believe that he is, and that he is a rewarder of them that diligently seek him."* (Hebrew 11:6)

B. As servants we are subject to **God's will**.

> *"And why call ye me, Lord, Lord, and do not the things which I say?."* (Luke 6:46)

C. We are all assigned tasks in **God's program**.

> *"And he that reapeth receiveth wages, and gathereth fruit unto life eternal: that both he that soweth and he that reapeth may rejoice together. And herein is that saying true, One soweth, and another reapeth."* (John 4:36-37)

Our time to rest will come, but now it is time to work.

Lesson 7-1
Application

1. Why are we to be humble rather than proud of what we do for God?

2. What part does faith have in serving God?

3. Why are some people proud of what they have done for God?

4. Why do we deserve nothing for serving God?

5. What difference has faith played in your Christian walk?

Lesson 7-2

Parable of the Ten Minas
(Ten Pounds)

Luke 19:11-27

Luke 19:11-27

¹¹ And as they heard these things, He added and spake a parable, because he was nigh to Jerusalem, and because they thought that the kingdom of God should immediately appear.

¹² He said therefore, A certain nobleman went into a far country to receive for himself a kingdom, and to return.

¹³ And he called his ten servants, and delivered them ten pounds, and said to them, Occupy until I come.

¹⁴ But his citizens hated him, and sent a message after him, saying, we will not have this man to reign over us.

¹⁵ And it came to pass, that when he was returned, having received the kingdom, then he commanded these servants to be called to him, to whom he had given the money, that he might know how much every man had gained by trading.

¹⁶ Then came the first, saying, Lord, your pound has gained ten pounds.

¹⁷ And he said to him, Well, you good servant: because thou has been faithful in a very little, have you authority over ten cities.

¹⁸ And the second came, saying, Lord, your pound has gained five pounds.

¹⁹ *And he said likewise to him, Be you also over five cities.*

²⁰ *And another came, saying, Lord, behold, here is your pound, which I have kept laid up in a napkin:*

²¹ *For I feared you, because you are an austere man: you took up that you laid not down, and reaped that you did not sow.*

²² *And he said to him, out of your own mouth will I judge you, you wicked servant. You knew that I was an austere man, taking up that I laid not down, and reaping that I did not sow:*

²³ *Wherefore then gave not you my money into the bank, that at my coming I might have required mine own with usury?*

²⁴ *And he said to them that stood by, Take from him the pound, and give it to him that has ten pounds.*

²⁵ *(And they said to him, Lord, he has ten pounds.)*

²⁶ *For I say to you, that to every one which has shall be given; and from him that has not, even that he has shall be taken away from him.*

²⁷ *But those mine enemies, which would not that I should reign over them, bring hither, and slay them before me.*

Lesson 7-2

One of the great expectations of the followers of Jesus was that the kingdom of God would immediately be established. This parable clarifies the sequence of events after the Lord's death. It also teaches that this life is a time for service (see previous "Parable of Obedient Servant", Lesson 5-1). Those who serve faithfully will be rewarded, and those who fail to serve will suffer loss.

What can we learn about our opportunity to serve God and God's program for the ages?

I. Christ's **promise** to return. (vv.11-12)

    A. The "nobleman" represents Jesus Christ.

> *"And when he had spoken these things, while they beheld, he was taken up; and a cloud received him out of their sight. And while they looked steadfastly toward heaven as he went up, behold, two men stood by them in white apparel; Which also said, Ye men of Galilee, why stand ye gazing up into heaven? this same Jesus, which is taken up from you into heaven, shall so come in like manner as ye have seen him go into heaven."* (Acts 1:9-11)

    B. His return will be **seen** by all.

    C. His return will take place on the **Mount of Olives**.

> *"And his feet shall stand in that day upon the mount of Olives, which is before Jerusalem on the east, and the mount of Olives shall cleave in the midst thereof toward the east and toward the west, and there shall be a very great valley; and half of the mountain shall remove toward the north, and half of it toward the south."* (Zechariah 14:4)

II. Christ's **Command.** "Occupy until I come." (v.13)

A. He gave them **money** which represents "opportunity for service".
A "pound" literally is a "mina" which equals one hundred drachma, a little more than three months' salary.

B. He gave them **responsibility**, commanding them to "occupy".
A concept that mature Christians embrace personal accountability.

> *"Moreover it is required in stewards that a man be found faithful."*
> (1 Corinthians 4:2)

> *"So then everyone of us shall give account of himself to God."*
> (Romans 14:12)

> *"Every man's work shall be made manifest: for the day shall declare it... If any man's work abide which he hath built thereupon, he shall receive a reward. If any man's work shall be burned, he shall suffer loss."*
> (I Corinthians 3:13-15)

III. Christ's **Return**, Reckoning and **Reward.** (vv.15-26)
Only three servants are mentioned. Each was given one pound (mina), thus each had equal opportunity.

A. The First Servant. (vv. 16-17)

1. His faithfulness resulted in a ten-fold return.
2. The Master's commendation was "*Well, thou good servant*" (v.17)
3. His reward: ten cities to rule.

B. The Second Servant. (vv.18-19)

1. His faithfulness resulted in five-fold return.
2. The Master's commendation was *"Well, thou good servant"* (v.18)
3. His reward: five cities to rule.

C. The Third Servant. (vv.20-26) Note the wicked servant's excuses.

1. *"I feared thee."* When you fear you respond without faith.
2. The Master's displeasure. Condemnation. *"wicked servant."* (v.21)
3. The servant's complaint. *"You take up what you don't sow."* (v.22)
4. The Master's response. He reminded the wicked servant of his responsibility and accountability. He takes the charge against himself, and tells the servant that, if he really believed that, he should have acted upon that knowledge. The fact that he received "judgment" suggests that he was lost. The first faithful servant received the reward that the wicked servant had lost. (vv.24-26)

> *"A good man out of the good treasure of the heart bringeth forth good things: and an evil man out of the evil treasure bringeth forth evil things. But I say unto you, that every idle word that men shall speak, they shall give account thereof in the day*

of judgment. For by thy words thou shalt be justified, and by thy words thou shalt be condemned." (Matthew 12:35-37)

IV. Christ Enemies **Destroyed.** (vv.14, 27)

A. Citizens represent "Unbelievers".
Those who should have received Christ, rejected Him. It is the same attitude of the world today.

"We will not have this man to reign over us." (v.14)

"As I live, saith the Lord, every knee shall bow to Me and every tongue shall confess to God." (Romans 14:11)

"And He hath on his vesture and on His thigh, a name written King of Kings, and Lord of Lords". (Revelation 19:16)

"And the remnant were slain with the sword of him that sat upon the horse, which sword proceeded out of his mouth..." (v.21)

B. Christ will have **his way.** (v.27)

"As I live, saith the Lord, every knee shall bow to me and every tongue shall confess to God." (Romans 14:11)

C. Christ's enemies will be totally **destroyed**.

"For he must reign, till he hath put all enemies under his feet." (1 Corinthians 15:25)

V. Some Observations.

    A. We demonstrate saving faith by using what God has given us for his glory.

    B. We are all responsible to use what God has given us.

    C. The first servant received what the evil servant misused.

Each of us has a limited time, an opportunity to serve God. Those who refuse to use the talents and opportunities they are given by God are disobedient at best, and lost at worst.

Lesson 7-2
Application

1. Will we all receive the same reward in heaven?

2. What are you doing with your "pound"?

3. How are you serving God?

4. What should you be doing now in your Christian walk of service?

5. What have you learned from this parable?

Lesson 7-3

The Parable of the Vineyard Laborers

Matthew 20:1-16

Matthew 20:1-16

¹ For the kingdom of heaven is like unto a man that is an householder, which went out early in the morning to hire laborers into his vineyard.

² And when he had agreed with the laborers for a penny a day, he sent them into his vineyard.

³ And he went out about the third hour, and saw others standing idle in the marketplace,

⁴ And said to them; Go ye also into the vineyard, and whatsoever is right I will give you. And they went their way.

⁵ Again he went out about the sixth and ninth hour, and did likewise.

⁶ And about the eleventh hour he went out, and found others standing idle, and saith unto them, Why stand you here all the day idle?

⁷ They say unto him, Because no man hath hired us. He saith unto them, Go ye also into the vineyard; and whatsoever is right, that shall you receive.

⁸ So when even was come, the lord of the vineyard saith to his steward, Call the laborers, and give them their hire, beginning from the last to the first.

⁹ And when they came that were hired about the eleventh hour, they received every man a penny.

^{10} But when the first came, they supposed that they should have received more; and they likewise received every man a penny.

^{11} And when they had received it, they murmured against the land owner of the house,

^{12} Saying, These last have labored but one hour, and thou have made them equal unto us, which have borne the burden and heat of the day.

^{13} But he answered one of them, and said, Friend, I do you no wrong: did not you agree with me for a penny?

^{14} Take that this is, and go your way: I will give unto this last, even as to you.

^{15} Is it not lawful for me to do what I will with mine own? Is your eye evil, because I am good?

^{16} So the last shall be first, and the first last: for many be called, but few chosen.

Lesson 7-3

Peter had asked the Lord an interesting question:

> "Behold, we have forsaken all, and followed thee; what shall we have therefore?"
> (Matthew 19:27)

Or simply expressed, "What's in it for me?"

Many people serve with the expectation of a great reward. Our service to God should be based on our love for God, and not on what we believe, on what God will owe us.

> "For the love of Christ constraineth us."
> (2 Corinthians 5:14)

I. The symbols in this parable about the Vineyard Workers.

    A. The Householder is the **Lord Jesus Christ**. He is the one who owns the vineyard.

    B. The laborers are the **believers**.

    C. The Penny represents **rewards** (salvation). A day's wage in Jesus time. It was the same pay a Roman soldier received.

    D. The hours represent different times of **service**, and or salvation.
Some of us are saved at different times of life. Others are saved, but they do not actively serve the Lord until they mature in their faith and commitment. Consider the times the laborers were hired. In Roman times, the hours were calculated from the sunrise.

        1. Third hour. 9:00 AM. morning.
        2. Sixth hour. 12:00 PM. noon.
        3. Ninth hour. 3:00 PM. afternoon.
        4. Eleventh hour. 5:00 PM. sunset.

II. The **importance** of Vineyards.

    A. A **common crop** in Israel.

        1. Vineyards were the source of one of the primary crops in Israel. Because of the people's familiarity with the vineyard, it was easily relatable to everyone.
        2. Vineyards had a wine press, commonly made by digging into the sides of a hill. There were two receptacles. Grapes were thrown into the smaller upper trench and trodden down by

men. The juices then ran down into the larger receptacle or cistern below.

3. Vineyards usually also had a tower in which to keep watch over the fields. These towers were built for the keeper of the vineyard, to guard against thieves, and animals (especially foxes). The towers were about fifteen to twenty feet high.

B. A **symbol** of the nation of Israel.
This symbol is still used on coins, stamps, and decorations in Israel. Isaiah 5:1-7 is a wonderful song about the God's love of the vineyard and the nation of Judah.

III. What we can learn about **serving** God.

A. God calls every believer to service.

> "That the man of God may be perfect, thoroughly furnished unto all good works." (2 Timothy 3:17)

B. Some believers start later than others.

C. There is **always work** to be done.

> "Say not ye, There are yet four months, and then cometh harvest? behold, I say unto you, Lift up your eyes, and look on the fields; for they are white already to harvest." (John 4:35)

D. God **rewards** as He wishes.

> "And, behold, I come quickly; and my reward is with me, to give every

man according as his work shall be."
(Revelation 22:12)

E. Everyone received what they were **promised**.

"For God is not unrighteous to forget your work and labor of love, which ye have shewed toward his name, in that ye have ministered to the saints, and do minister." (Hebrews 6:10)

F. God rewards as **He wills**. (v.13-15) Don't make bargains with God. Trust him to be fair and generous. He will always do what is right.

Lesson 7-3
Application

1. When were you saved?

2. How are you serving God now?

3. Do you ever feel jealous of what others are doing for the Lord?

4. Is God unfair?

LESSON 7-4

THE PARABLE OF THE TALENTS

Matthew 25:14-30

Matthew 25:14-30

14 For the kingdom of heaven is as a man travelling into a far country, who called his own servants, and delivered to them his goods.

15 And to one he gave five talents, to another two, and to another one; to every man according to his several abilities; and straightway took his journey.

16 Then he that had received the five talents went and traded with the same, and made them other five talents.

17 And likewise he that had received two, he also gained other two.

18 But he that had received one went and dug in the earth, and hid his lord's money.

19 After a long time the lord of those servants came, and reckoned with them.

20 And so he that had received five talents came and brought other five talents, saying, Lord, you delivered to me five talents: behold, I have gained beside them five talents more.

21 His lord said unto him, Well done, thou good and faithful servant: thou hast been faithful over a few things, I will make you ruler over many things: enter you into the joy of thy lord.

22 He also that had received two talents came and said, Lord, you delivered to me two talents: behold, I have gained two other talents beside them.

23 *His lord said to him, Well done, good and faithful servant; you hast been faithful over a few things, I will make you ruler over many things: enter you into the joy of thy lord.*

24 *Then he which had received the one talent came and said, Lord, I knew you that thou art a hard man, reaping where you hast not sown, and gathering where you hast not strawed:*

25 *And I was afraid, and went and hid my talent in the earth: lo, there you have that is mine.*

26 *His lord answered and said unto him, You wicked and slothful servant, you knew that I reap where I sowed not, and gather where I have not strawed:*

27 *You ought therefore to have put my money to the exchangers, and then at my coming I should have received mine own with usury.*

28 *Take therefore the talent from him, and give it unto him which hath ten talents.*

29 *For unto every one that has shall be given, and he shall have abundance: but from him that has not shall be taken away even that which he has.*

30 *And cast you the unprofitable servant into outer darkness: there shall be weeping and gnashing of teeth.*

Lesson 7-4

After visiting the temple (Matthew 24), Jesus taught this parable on the Mount of Olives to his disciples. The theme was the "kingdom of heaven", where Jesus gave parables emphasizing His second coming. This parable deals with personal accountability and the Master departs and leaves talents for his "servants" at the end of the age.

I. Keys to **Understanding** this Parable.

    A. The "**kingdom of heaven**" comprises of all professing believers.

    B. The "**servants**" are those who claim to be serving God, whether saved or lost.

    C. The "**Man**" represents Christ.

    D. The "**talents**" represents opportunity.

II. Some things to consider of what each servant was given.

    A. What we have is **not ours**. (v.14)
    It was not uncommon for a master to take a journey and entrust his goods and property to his servants.

> "*The earth is the Lord's, and the fullness thereof; the world and they that dwell therein.*" (Psalm 24:1)

    He has the rights, but each of us has the responsibility.

    B. We are given what we **can handle**. (v.15)
    The **values** were great. A talent is about six thousand denarii, (twenty years for a common laborer).

    C. The **opportunity** varied.

    D. While we all possess spiritual gifts the moment of salvation, we are all different and have various gifts to minister to each other.

> *"The selfsame Spirit, dividing to every man severally as he will."*
> (1 Corinthians 12:11)

E. What we do **reveals** what we think about ourselves and God. (v.19)

1. We excuse ourselves by saying I can't do as much as someone else, so we do **little to nothing**.
2. We act as though God is asking **too much**.
3. We pretend that God doesn't expect **anything from us**.

III. An accounting of the **Servants**. (vv.20-23)

A. The **Faithful** Servants.

1. Both **used** what they were given. (vv.20,22)
2. Both **received** the same reward. (vv.20,22)
3. Both were **commended** and given greater responsibility. (vv.21,23)
   This commendation has three elements:

   - **Affirmation.** *"Well done."*
   - **Promotion.** *"I will make thee ruler over many things."*
   - **Celebration.** *"Enter into the joy of thy Lord."*

B. The **unfruitful** servant. (vv.24-30)

1. He complained about his responsibility. (v.24)
   A faulty view of God leads to **complaining**. He thought he was playing it safe by digging a hold in the ground. He dug the hole for himself.

2. He purposely **neglected** his responsibility. (v.25)
He knew what to do, but **disobeyed**.
3. He was **condemned** and called "*wicked and slothful.*" (v.26)
4. He was **reprimanded** for his neglect. (vv.27-29).
5. He was **cast** into outer darkness. (v.30)
This is a picture of judgment, which is reserved for the lost.

We are not to compare our ministries or results with others. We are only required to be faithful.

"*Moreover it is required in stewards, that a man be found faithful.*"
(1 Corinthians 4:2)

A distinguishing mark of a true Christian is service and giving. A lack of service suggests a heart where Jesus doesn't live. Using what you have brings honor to God. Avoiding your opportunity brings shame. Are you saved? Are you serving God?

Lesson 7-4
Application

1. Are you using the talents that God has given you?

   How?

2. Why must we not judge our results with other believers?

3. Will we someday have to give an account to God for how we lived our lives?

4. Will our rewards in heaven be based on our faithfulness in this life?

5. What, if anything, do you plan to do different in serving God?

CHAPTER EIGHT

PARABLES OF THE NATION OF ISRAEL AND REJECTION OF THE MESSIAH: THE LAST WEEK OF JESUS' MINISTRY

Lesson 8-1   New Cloth   Matt 9:16
Mark 2:21;
Luke 5:36

Lesson 8-2   New Wine   Matt 9:17
Mark 2:22;
Luke 5:37-39

Lesson 8-3   Barren Fig Tree   Luke 13:6-9

Lesson 8-4   Great Supper   Luke 14:16-24

Lesson 8-5   Two Sons   Matt 21:28-32

Lesson 8-6   Wicked Tenants   Matt 21:33-45
                             Mark 12:1-12
                             Luke 20:9-19

Lesson 8-7   Fig Tree   Matt 24:32-35
                             Mark 13:28-31
                             Luke 21:29-33

Lesson 8-1

The Parable of the New Cloth

AND

Lesson 8-2

The Parable of New Wine in Old Bottles

Matthew 9:16-17; Mark 2:21-22; Luke 5:36-39

These two parables are grouped together because they are closely related.

I. The Settings.
   In the Old Testament, God speaks of the covenant of marriage to convey the loving relationship of God to the nation of Israel.

> *"For thy Maker is thine husband."* (Isaiah 54:5)

The New Testament also shows God's relationship to believers is similar to marriage.

> *"Blessed are they which are called unto the marriage supper of the Lamb"*. (Revelation 19:9)

So, what can we learn from these passages?

A. Jesus' **presence** on earth was like a wedding feast with Jesus the bridegroom. It was a time of **joy**, not sorrow.

B. Jesus' **departure** would be the appropriate time of fasting and **sorrow.**

LESSON 8-1

THE PARABLE OF THE NEW CLOTH

Matthew 9:16; Mark 2:21; Luke 5:36

Mark 2:21

²¹ *No man also sews a piece of new cloth on an old garment: else the new piece that filled it up takes away from the old, and the rent is made worse.*

Lesson 8-1

I. The Parable of the **New Cloth:**

    A. Old Cloth signifies the Old Covenant Law of Moses.

    B. New Cloth signifies the New Covenant of Christianity.

New cloth has not been properly treated or shrunk. If used to patch a tear in an older garment, it would eventually shrink and make a worse tear.

Jesus' message of the kingdom of God is incompatible with the present condition of Judaism.

The Old Covenant was unable to secure righteousness and was too damaged to be fixed by adding "new cloth" to restore it. Judaism cannot be fixed by adding Christianity to it. It is new in its emphasis of grace rather than law. Jesus came to bring a new way of life and not patch up the old.

LESSON 8-2

THE PARABLE OF THE NEW WINE

Matt 9:17; Mark 2:22; Luke 5:37-39

Mark 2:22

22 *And no man puts new wine into old bottles: else the new wine doth burst the bottles, and the wine is spilled, and the bottles will be marred: but new wine must be put into new bottles.*

Lesson 8-2

I. Wineskins (bottles) were used to hold liquid. Usually, wineskins were made out of goat. The fermentation of the new wine would cause it to break out of old wineskins. This is why new wine was placed in new wineskins. If left alone, it would eventually ferment, and then rot, and turn into vinegar.

> *"Knowing that a man is not justified by the works of the law: for by the faith of Jesus Christ, even we have believed in Jesus Christ, that we might be justified by the faith of Christ, and not by the works of the law; for by the works of the law shall no flesh be justified."* (Galatians 2:16)

> *"I do not frustrate the grace of God: for if righteousness come by the law, then Christ is dead in vain."* (Galatians 2:21)

"Wherefore the law was our schoolmaster to bring us unto Christ, that we might be justified by faith. But after that faith is come, we are no longer under a schoolmaster." (Galatians 3:24-25)

II. Observations on the incompatibility of Judaism with Christianity:

A. The new wine of the New Covenant would never fit within the constraints of the Old Covenant of Judaism.

B. Only a new covenant ratified with blood would be sufficient to provide the Gospel of Salvation to the world.

C. Judaism and Christianity are incompatible.

D. Some churches/people resist anything new and become irrelevant in sharing their faith.

E. Some churches/people accept anything that comes along, and in the process, loses what should be preserved.

Lessons 8-1 and 8-2
Application

1. Why did the Jews of Jesus' day have difficulty in believing Jesus' message?

2. Why can't Christianity and Judaism mix?

3. Why is Christianity superior to Judaism?

4. What is the danger of tradition?

5. What are some new ways for you to share the Gospel personally?

   As a church?

LESSON 8-3

PARABLE OF THE BARREN FIG TREE

Luke 13:6-9

Luke 13:6-9

6 He spoke also this parable; A certain man had a fig tree planted in his vineyard; and he came and sought fruit thereon, and found none.

7 Then said he unto the dresser of his vineyard, Behold, these three years I come seeking fruit on this fig tree, and find none: cut it down; why cumbereth it the ground?

8 And he answering said unto him, Lord, let it alone this year also, till I shall dig about it, and dung it:

9 And if it bear fruit, well: and if not, then after that thou shalt cut it down.

Lesson 8-3

This parable deals with the response of the nation of Israel and their national response to Jesus as the Messiah. It was given in response to the Lord being informed that some Galileans were killed by Pilate while they were offering sacrifices to God, and the collapse of the Tower in Siloam where eighteen men were killed, (vv.1-5). This tower was near the pool of Siloam south of the temple.

Jesus' response was to call for repentance.

"Whereas ye know not what shall be on the morrow. For what is your life? It is even a vapour, that appeareth for a little time, and then vanisheth away." (James 4:14)

This is obviously a warning to repent while there is still time.

I. Understanding the **Symbols**.

A. **Man**.
In the New Testament parables, the man usually represents the **Lord Jesus**. He is the one in charge and to whom we are accountable.

B. **Fig Tree.**
The fig tree has historically represented the nation of **Israel** and has appeared on coinage. In Jeremiah 24, figs both good and bad represent all the people of Israel. The fact that this fig tree is planted in a vineyard, another symbol of the nation of Israel is an indication that the fig tree also represents Israel.

C. **Vineyard.**
The vineyard represents Israel.

"For the vineyard of the Lord of hosts is the house of Israel, and the men of Judah his pleasant plant: and he looked for judgment, but behold oppression; for righteousness, but behold a cry." (Isaiah 5:7)

D. **No fruit.**

1. The whole idea of planting is to harvest. The law was very clear concerning the process for trees.

> "And when ye shall come into the land, and shall have planted all manner of trees for food, then ye shall count the fruit thereof as uncircumcised: three years shall it be as uncircumcised unto you; it shall not be eaten of. But in the fourth year all the fruit thereof shall be holy to praise the Lord withal. And in the fifth year shall ye eat of the fruit thereof, that it may yield unto you the increase thereof. I am the Lord your God".
> (Leviticus 19:23-25)

2. Fruit from newly planted trees could not be eaten for three years. The fourth year was Holy unto the Lord, and belonged to him. The fifth year was for the farmer. This man waits until the seventh year and still had no fruit. No wonder he wanted it cut down.
3. The lack of fruit represented a lack of faith by the people of Israel.

II. Jesus' **Warning**.

A. Everything necessary had been done for **Israel's repentance**. Like the fig tree, they were well watered and dunged.

1. God gave Jesus three years of ministry, then Israel rejected their opportunity to receive Christ.
2. Dung symbolizes the Gospel message. God waited about forty more years, until 70 A.D., when the Romans, under General Titus, destroyed Jerusalem and the Temple.
3. God gave a clear message about repentance.

B. **Rejection of Christ**, representing the "cutting down" or judgment. This is comparable to Matthew 3:7-12. In sparing John the Baptist's forerunner ministry, the Pharisees and Sadducees were warned about the lack of spiritual fruit in their lives and the coming judgment.

III. Some **Observations.**

A. If the Galileans were destroyed for no apparent reason while they were sacrificing to God in the Temple area, what can be expected for a nation that **willfully rejected** their Messiah in the day of their judgment?

B. We are expected to bear **spiritual fruit**.

> "But the fruit of the "Spirit is love, joy, peace, longsuffering, gentleness, goodness, faith, Meekness, temperance: against such there is no law." (Galatians 5:22-23)

C. The Lord is **patient**, but patience eventually ends.

> *"The Lord is not slack concerning his promise, as some men count slackness; but is longsuffering to us-ward, not willing that any should perish, but that all should come to repentance."* (2 Peter 3:9)

Lesson 8-3
Application

1. Are you bearing fruit in your life?

   Why or why not?

2. What are you doing for the Lord?

3. What can you do to be a fruit-bearing Christian?

LESSON 8-4

THE PARABLE OF THE GREAT SUPPER

Luke 14:16-24

Luke 14:16-24

16 *Then said a man to him, A certain man made a great supper, and bade many:*

17 *And sent his servant at supper time to say to them that were bidden, Come; for all things are now ready.*

18 *And they all with one consent began to make excuse. The first said unto him, I have bought a piece of ground, and I must needs go and see it: I pray you have me excused.*

19 *And another said, I have bought five yoke of oxen, and I go to prove them: I pray you have me excused.*

20 *And another said, I have married a wife, and therefore I cannot come.*

21 *So that servant came, and showed his lord these things. Then the master of the house being angry said to his servant, Go out quickly into the streets and lanes of the city, and bring in hither the poor, and the maimed, and the lame, and the blind.*

22 *And the servant said, Lord, it is done as thou hast commanded, and yet there is room.*

23 *And the lord said unto the servant, Go out into the highways and hedges, and compel them to come in, that my house may be filled.*

24 *For I say unto you, That none of those men which were bidden shall taste of my supper.*

Lesson 8-4

In the Middle East, men of wealth and nobility would generally prepare great feasts and meals for their associates. Two calls would be given for the planned feast. The first call was an invitation with the announcement to make ready all that was necessary in order to come in short notice. The second call was to come at once as the feast was now ready and those invited should come at once. This social custom of hospitality is still practiced by Bedouins today. What can we learn from this parable?

I. The **Invitation.** (v.16-17)
   The Great Supper is a picture of salvation for the Jews. The Lord, of course, is Jesus Christ. Jesus came primarily to the Jews to offer them the kingdom. Consider what the Lord did.

   A. The greatest provision: **salvation**.
      The Lord offers salvation to those who should have responded and received it.

   B. The greatest person: **Jesus Christ**.
      The offer of salvation was given by the greatest person who ever lived. When your reject Jesus, you insult the greatest being in the universe.

   C. In response to the statement:

      "Blessed is he that shall eat bread in the Kingdom of God." (v.15)

II. **The Story.** *"A certain man made a great supper."* (v.16)

A. The Certain Man represents **Christ**.
This man is unknown to the reader, but he was of great authority and wealth.

B. The Great Supper represents **Salvation**.
Clearly, it was a lavish affair which all could enjoy.

C. Invited Guests represents the **Jews**.
All the persons of the same social order and fellowship could enjoy.

D. The poor, maimed, and blind represented the **Social Outcasts/Gentiles**.
Those who normally did not fit, or were unacceptable were also invited.

III. The **Preoccupation** (or Excuse).
The Lord had given out invitations, and then on the night of the Great Supper, he had sent out his servants. These servants represent those who faithfully serve the Lord, and spread His word. Unfortunately, those invited refused to come. Look at their excuses.

A. *"I have bought a piece of ground, and I must needs go see it."* (v.18)

1. It is foolish to purchase land without seeing it. Once bought, it is unlikely to disappear.
2. The wickedness of this excuse is that dinners were usually held at night, when the sun was going down. You do not examine land at night.

B. "*I have bought five yoke of oxen, and I go to prove them.*" (v.19)

    1. Again, it is too late to prove (or test) oxen once you have purchased them.
    2. No thinking person would send expensive oxen to plow at night where they might stumble and injure themselves.

C. "*I have married a wife, and therefore I cannot come.*" (v.20)

    1. No earthly relative is more important than God.
    2. The husband is responsible for the spiritual direction of the family:

> "*But seek ye first the kingdom of God, and His righteousness; and all these things shall be added unto you.*" (Matthew 6:33)

> "*If any man come to me, and hate not his father, and mother, and wife, and children, and brethren, and sisters, yea, and his own life also, he cannot be my disciple.*" (Luke 14:26)

Eternal life should be our highest priority. Our relationship even to family is secondary.

> "*And ye will not come to me, that ye might have life.*" (John 5:40)

IV. The **Indignation**. (vv.21-24)

When the Lord was told of the ungracious responses to his final invitation, a several events happened.

A. The Lord's anger was kindled. (v.21)
Excuses bring the wrath of God:

> "*Of how much sorer punishment, suppose ye, shall he be thought worthy, who hath trodden under foot the Son of God, and hath counted the blood of the covenant, wherewith he was sanctified, an unholy thing, and hath done despite unto the Spirit of grace?*" (Hebrews 10:29)

B. Excuses Result in Lost Opportunity. (v.21)

1. Service.
2. Purpose.
3. Contentment.
4. Salvation.

C. The Lord invites others. (vv.21-23)
There is still room. The servants were commanded to fill the man's house with guests. The Lord disinvited those who rejected his invitation. These "others" were those who normally would have been rejected as unworthy of being invited. (v.24)

1. Highways.
2. Public roads.
3. Hedges.

Enclosed fields where common field hands were hired to plant, cut, and trim gardens and trees.

V. The **Presentation**.

Look what ignoring the Lord's invitation costs:

A. **Salvation**.

Salvation ignored is salvation lost.

> *"And the Lord said, My spirit shall not always strive with man, for that he also is flesh: yet his days shall be an hundred and twenty years."* (Genesis 6:3)

> *"behold, now is the accepted time; behold, now is the day of Salvation."* (2 Corinthians 6:2)

B. **Blessings**.

God's supper gives contentment and rest:

> *"Blessed are they which are called unto the marriage supper of the Lamb."* (Revelation 19:9)

God's call for the "Great Supper" is genuine. The time to come is now. Those who willfully ignore God's call, do so at their own risk. The nation of Israel rejected Christ's invitation.

Lesson 8-4
Application

1. Why do you think the Jews, as a nation, rejected Christ?

2. What did the Jews rejection of Christ do for you?

3. What is our responsibility in this day and age toward those who are unsaved?

4. How do you plan to reach those who are lost?

5. What effort will you make in your attempts to reach others?

LESSON 8-5

PARABLE OF THE TWO SONS

Matthew 21:28-32

Matthew 21:28-32

28 But what think you? A certain man had two sons; and he came to the first, and said, Son, go work today in my vineyard.

29 He answered and said, I will not: but afterward he repented, and went.

30 And he came to the second, and said likewise. And he answered and said, I go, sir: and went not.

31 Whether of them twain did the will of his father? They say unto him, The first. Jesus saith to them, Verily I say to you, That the publicans and the harlots go into the kingdom of God before you.

32 For John came to you in the way of righteousness, and you believed him not: but the publicans and the harlots believed him: and you, when you had seen it, repented not afterward, that you might believe him.

Lesson 8-5

After Jesus' triumphant entry recorded in Matthew 21:5-9, He went into the temple and overthrew the money changers' tables. (v.12) In the last week of his life, and after Jesus is challenged by the chief priests and elders about His authority, (v.23), he gives this parable of the two sons.

I. The **Story.** *"A certain man had two sons".*
As always, Jesus gives a story in which each son represents a type of person, and their response to the Father

    A. The **first son** represents, *"publicans, sinners, and harlots."* (v.31)

    B. The **second son** represents "The Priests, Pharisees, Sadducees, and Scribes". (v.32)

    C. The **man** represents God the Father.

    D. The **vineyard** represents those Jews who repented and entered into "the kingdom of God." (v.31)

II. The **Father**'s claim and desire. (v.28)

    A. "**Son**".
As a child of God, we should willingly work and do God's will. There are many who claim to be God's child, yet live like the devil's child.

> *"For so is the will of God, that with well doing ye may put to silence the ignorance of foolish men."* (1 Peter 2:15)

    B. "**Work**". (v.28)
God desires that we work for him. We must work while the opportunity is still available. Consider these verses:

> *"See then that ye walk circumspectly, not as fools, but as wise, Redeeming the time, because the days are evil. Wherefore be ye not unwise, but*

understanding what the will of the Lord is." (Ephesians 5:15-17)

"I must work the works of him that sent me, while it is day: the night cometh, when no man can work." (John 9:4)

C. **"Today."** (v.28)
The urgency is now. Jesus ministered to the Samaritan woman.

"Say not ye, there are yet four months, and then cometh harvest? behold, I say unto you, Lift up your eyes, and look on the fields; for they are white already to harvest." (John 4:35)

There is plenty of work to do in God's kingdom.

III. Comparison of the Two Sons and their responses. (vv.29-30)

A. The **First Son.** (v.29)
He refused to go, but later repented and went. His was an open sin of rebellion.

"But be ye doers of the word, and not hearers only, deceiving your own selves." (James 1:22)

B. The **Second Son**. (v.30)
He promised to go, but did not. His sin was the sin of disobedience.

"And why call ye me, Lord, Lord, and do not the things which I say?" (Luke 6:46)

Christ told us:

> "*If ye love me, keep my commandments.*" (John 14:15)

IV. The question **Christ asked**:

> "*Which of them twain did the will of his father? (v.31)*

A. It was a simple question.
The question made the critics involved in the parable.

B. It was a searching question.
The question made the critics examine their own lives in relationship to God's will.

V. The Real Issue: **Repentance**. (v.32)
The ministry of John the Baptist was disregarded by them, but it was believed by publicans and harlots. They repented but these religious zealots did not. What can we learn?

A. Not those who merely say, but those who do, are **truly saved**.

B. The wicked are more open to **change** than the self-righteous.

C. It is **dangerous** to see ourselves as better and more righteous than others.

D. **Substituting** religious practice for genuine repentance is dangerous.

E. The self-righteous and self-satisfied are in greater danger than the openly wicked.

> "*Because thou sayest, I am rich, and increased with goods, and have need of nothing; and knowest not that thou art wretched, and miserable, and poor, and blind, and naked.*" (Revelation 3:17)

Lesson 8-5
Application

1. Why is it important that we be honest about our spiritual state?

2. What should our response be to those who are social outcasts?

3. Do you obey God's Word or just give lip service?

4. Are you content in your spiritual walk?

5. How do you plan to reach the "down and out"?

Lesson 8-6

Parable of the Wicked Tenants

(Householder's Vineyard)

Matthew 21:33-45; Mark 12:1-12; Luke 20:9-19

Matthew 21:33-45

33 Hear another parable: There was a certain householder, which planted a vineyard, and hedged it round about, and dug a winepress in it, and built a tower, and let it out to husbandmen, and went into a far country:

34 And when the time of the fruit drew near, he sent his servants to the husbandmen, that they might receive the fruits of it.

35 And the husbandmen took his servants, and beat one, and killed another, and stoned another.

36 Again, he sent other servants more than the first: and they did to them likewise.

37 But last of all he sent to them his son, saying, they will reverence my son.

38 But when the husbandmen saw the son, they said among themselves, This is the heir; come, let us kill him, and let us seize on his inheritance.

39 And they caught him, and cast him out of the vineyard, and slew him.

40 When the lord therefore of the vineyard cometh, what will he do to those husbandmen?

41 They say to him, He will miserably destroy those wicked men, and will let out his vineyard to other

husbandmen, which shall render him the fruits in their seasons.

⁴² Jesus saith unto them, Did you never read in the scriptures, The stone which the builders rejected, the same is become the head of the corner: this is the Lord's doing, and it is marvelous in our eyes?

⁴³ Therefore say I to you, The kingdom of God shall be taken from you, and given to a nation bringing forth the fruits thereof.

⁴⁴ And whosoever shall fall on this stone shall be broken: but on whomsoever it shall fall, it will grind him to powder.

⁴⁵ And when the chief priests and Pharisees had heard his parables, they perceived that he spake of them.

Lesson 8-6

This parable deals with the nationwide rejection of Jesus as the Christ. The symbols used in this parable are obvious.

I. The **symbols** of this parable explained:

A. The vineyard represents **Israel**.

> *"For the vineyard of the Lord of hosts is the house of Israel, and the men of Judah his pleasant plant."* (Isaiah 5:7)

B. The landowner is **God**.
He is the one who owns the nation of Israel and everything else.

> *"For God is King of all the earth."* (Psalm 47:7)

"The earth is the Lord's, and the fullness thereof; the world, and they that dwell therein." (Psalm 24:1)

C. The servants were God's representatives who were sent to the nation of **Israel**. They were often mistreated, tortured, put on trial for cruelty and scourging, imprisonment, stoned, sawn asunder, slain by the sword, left destitute, afflicted, tormented, and wandering in the desert and mountains.
In other words, they were abused and treated badly.

D. The vinedressers (husbandmen) represents **Israel's leaders**. (vv.45-46) The amazing thing is that Jesus told them what they would do and even told them they would be successful and kill him.

E. The landowner's son is **Jesus**. He is the rightful heir.

II. The Vineyard.

A. **Expended** labor. (v.33)
The householder, God the Father, had done everything to prepare the land.

1. It was "planted": grape vines in place.
2. It was "hedged": usually a stone wall to keep out animals and intruders.
3. It was "digged": ground tilled and irrigated. A "tower" was built to watch over field, usually fifteen to twenty feet high.
4. Husbandmen (workers) were hired to keep the land.

B. **Exceptional** opportunity. (v.33)
These husbandmen had everything they needed to succeed and enjoy the land. As a Christian, you have everything you need to accomplish God's will.

> *"That the man of God may be perfect, thoroughly furnished unto all good works."* (2 Timothy 3:17)

C. **Expected** fruit. (v.34)
The time of harvest came and the house owner sent a servant for his share of the fruit. As Christians, our responsibility is apparent:

> *"For we are laborers together with God; ye are God's husbandry, ye are God's building."* (1 Corinthians 3:9)

D. **Exhibited** unthankfulness. (v.35-36)
Instead of faithfully responding to their duty, they ignored and mistreated God's servants.

> *"And the LORD God of their fathers sent to them by his messengers, rising up betimes, and sending; because he had compassion on his people, and on his dwelling place;*
>
> *But they mocked the messengers of God, and despised his words, and misused his prophets, until the wrath of the LORD arose against his people, till there was no remedy."* (2 Chronicles 36:15-16)

E. **Extreme** wickedness. (vv.36-39)
The Husbandmen Rebelled.

1. They mistreated the servants.
2. They killed the Son.
3. They sought to make the inheritance theirs.

After mistreating God's servants, these husbandmen killed the legitimate heir, Jesus Christ. God will not let their injustice go unpunished!

III. God's **Vengeance.** (vv.40-46)
Having rejected God and murdered his Son, the only remedy is judgment.

A. God's **patience** comes to an end.
The husbandmen are destroyed. While time may pass, God's judgment is certain. In 70 A.D., the Romans, under General Titus, destroyed Jerusalem. It has been estimated that more than one million (1,000,000) Jews perished from famine, disease, sword, and crucifixion.

> "The Lord is not slack concerning His promise, as some men count slackness; but is longsuffering to us-ward, not willing that any should perish, but that all should come to repentance." (2 Peter 3:9)

B. The Lord **judges**.

> "They shall put you out of the synagogues: yea, the time cometh, that whosoever killeth you will think that he doeth God service. And these things will they do unto you because

they have not known the Father, nor me." (John 16:2-3)

"In flaming fire taking vengeance on them that know not God, and that they obey not the gospel of our Lord Jesus Christ."
(2 Thessalonians 1:8)

C. New husbandmen are hired. Those who receive Christ will have the opportunity to **render fruit** at the harvest. (vv.41-44)

The lesson to you and me is that ignoring spiritual obligations results in unpleasant endings. For Christians, it will bring shame at the judgment seat of Christ. To the lost, it will bring eternal judgment in hell.

Lesson 8-6
Application

1. Why was the householder slow to deal with the husbandmen?

2. Why did the husbandmen (religious leaders) refuse to submit?

3. What does God's response to the religious leaders mean to you?

4. How do you know whether you are in a right relationship to God?

Lesson 8-7

The Parable of the Fig Tree

Budding Tree

Matt 24:32-35; Mark 13:28-31; Luke 21:29-33

Matthew 24:32-35

32 Now learn a parable of the fig tree; When his branch is yet tender, and puts forth leaves, you know that summer is nigh:

33 So likewise you, when you shall see all these things, know that it is near, even at the doors.

34 Verily I say unto you, This generation shall not pass, till all these things be fulfilled.

35 Heaven and earth shall pass away, but my words shall not pass away.

Lesson 8-7

Matthew 24 begins with a prediction of destruction of the temple in Jerusalem. The disciples ask these questions:

> *"When shall these things be? And what shall be the sign of thy coming, and of the end of the world?"* (v.3)

This parable in verses 32-35 deals with the events preceding the Second Coming of our Lord Jesus Christ.

The danger for Christians in our day is to focus on our present distress, and miss what God is doing in the world. Don't be worried about the future. It is in God's hands. Be ready when Jesus returns. Without Christ, everything appears troubled because only Christ, The Prince of Peace can bring peace to a troubled world.

Consider this article from the October 1857 edition of *Harper's Weekly*:

> "It is a gloomy moment in the history of our country. Not in the lifetime of most men has there been so much grave and deep apprehension; never has the future seemed so unpredictable as at this time. The domestic economic situation is in chaos. Our dollar is weak throughout the world. Prices are so high as to be utterly impossible. The political cauldron seethes and bubbles with uncertainty. It is a solemn moment of our troubles. No man can see the end."

This article appeared just four years before the start of the Civil War.

Jesus doesn't give a date for his return, but he does give us warning signs that the end is approaching.

The parable of the fig tree was given as part of the Mount of Olives discourse in Matthew 24, and was directed toward the Jewish believers.

I. The Parable of the **Fig Tree**. (vv.32-35)

    A. The **fig tree**. (v.32)
       Historically, the fig tree has represented the nation of Israel. When it sends forth leaves, summer is soon to follow. The idea is that the

signs mentioned in Matthew 24 are indications that Christ will soon return.

B. The **generation**. (v.34)
These are the people who see these things come to pass. It is a warning to be prepared.

C. The **words**. (v.35)
God's book and Christ's words are eternal. They have no expiration date.

II. The events of **Matthew 24**.

A. False prophets will be **pretending** to be Christ. (vv.4-5)

B. **Wars** and rumors of wars. (vv.6-7)
We have more wars now, throughout the world, than at any other time in history.

C. **Suffering** for being a Christian. (v.8-11)
It is estimated that more than one hundred Christian believers are killed every year for their faith. More are imprisoned, tortured, and mistreated.

D. **Coldness** concerning things of God. (vv.12-13)
People have taken their devotion for Christ and focused it on possessions and entertainment.

E. The **revealing** of "The Abomination of Desolation". (vv.15-20)
This is the Anti-Christ. He will enter the temple that should be built sometime in the future and declare himself to be God.

F. **False signs** and **wonders**. (vv.21-24)
The "False Prophet", who works with the Anti-Christ.

> "*and he doeth great wonders, so that he maketh fire com down from heaven on the earth in the sight of men. And deceiveth them that dwell on the earth by the means of those miracles which he had power to do in the sight of the beast.*" (Revelation 13:13-14)

G. Christ will come suddenly and **without warning.** (vv.25-28)

III. Some Practical Applications and Observations.

A. Israel will rise as a nation. This became a reality in 1948 when it was re-established.

B. The generation that sees all these events unfold in Matthew 24 is the last generation of Christ's return.

C. Be ready for Christ's return. Make sure of your salvation.

D. Tell others so they can be saved, and be ready as well.

Lesson 8-7
Application

1. Have you noticed any of the "signs" of Christ's return?

2. Why will some people's hearts turn away from God?

3. Are you living your life with the expectation of Christ's return?

   How?

CHAPTER NINE

Parables of The Lord's Return

Lesson 9-1   Watchful and Foolish   Luke 12:35-40
              Servants

Lesson 9-2   Shrewd and Unjust   Luke 16:1-13
              Steward

Lesson 9-3   Rich Man and Lazarus   Luke 16:19-31

Lesson 9-4   Absent Householder   Mark 13:34-37
              (Master's Return)

Lesson 9-5   Invitation to Wedding   Matt 22:1-14
              Feast (Wedding
              Garment)

Lesson 9-6   Ten Virgins   Matt 25:1-13

Lesson 9-7   Sheep and Goats   Matt 25:31-46

Lesson 9-1

Parable of the Watchful and Foolish Servants

Luke 12:35-48

Luke 12:35-48

35 *Let your loins be girded about, and your lights burning;*

36 *And you yourselves like unto men that wait for their lord, when he will return from the wedding; that when he comes and knocks, they may open unto him immediately.*

37 *Blessed are those servants, whom the lord when he comes shall find watching: verily I say unto you, that he shall gird himself, and make them to sit down to meat, and will come forth and serve them.*

38 *And if he shall come in the second watch, or come in the third watch, and find them so, blessed are those servants.*

39 *And know this, that if the good man of the house had known what hour the thief would come, he would have watched, and not have suffered his house to be broken through.*

40 *Be ye therefore ready also: for the Son of man comes at an hour when ye think not.*

41 *Then Peter said uno him, Lord, speakest thou this parable unto us, or even to all?*

42 *And the Lord said, Who then is that faithful and wise steward, whom his lord shall make ruler over his household, to give them their portion of meat in due season?*

⁴³ Blessed is that servant, whom his lord when he comes shall find so doing.

⁴⁴ Of a truth I say unto you, that he will make him ruler over all that he hath.

⁴⁵ But and if that servant says in his heart, My lord delays his coming; and shall begin to beat the menservants and maidens, and to eat and drink, and to be drunken;

⁴⁶ The lord of that servant will come in a day when he looks not for him, and at an hour when he is not aware, and will cut him in sunder, and will appoint him his portion with the unbelievers.

⁴⁷ And that servant, which knew his lord's will, and prepared not himself, neither did according to his will, shall be beaten with many stripes.

⁴⁸ But he that knew not, and did commit things worthy of stripes, shall be beaten with few stripes. For unto whomsoever much is given, of him shall be much required: and to whom men have committed much, of him they will ask the more.

Lesson 9-1

Many people make poor choices in regard to spiritual things because their focus is on the immediate and not the future. Once a believer thinks the Lord is not returning, they gets sloppy in their relationship with God. Our relationships with others are affected by our relationship with God. A healthy spiritual life is focused on the future while living in the present. To underscore this principle of focusing on the future, Jesus told this parable concerning his return.

After instructing his disciples to *"seek ye the kingdom of God."* (v.31) Jesus gives this parable of his return using the imagery of a wedding.

What is unusual about this return is that instead of the servants serving the master, the master serves the servants. In order to stress the importance of being prepared for his return, Jesus gave clear instruction on what we are expected to do.

I. The **Setting.**

    A. After warning about covetousness.

    B. After speaking to his disciples about seeking the kingdom of God first and trusting God to meet their needs. (v.31)

II. The **Story.**

> *"Blessed are those servants, whom the Lord when he cometh shall find watching."* (v.37)

    A. The Lord. Jesus Christ.

    B. The faithful servant. Obedient believer.

    C. The unfaithful servant. Disobedient "believer".

    D. The indifferent servant. Immature believer.

III. The Three **Servants.**

    A. The **Faithful Servant**. (vv.35-44)
    What is unusual about this return is that instead of the servants serving the master, the master serves the servants. In order to stress the importance of his return, Jesus gives clear instructions on what we should be doing.

1. **Wait.** (v.35) *"loins be girded"*. Servants were "dressed", and "watching and waiting" will be rewarded. Note that the faithful servants who are doing their job *"lights burning"* (v.35).

   > *"So then every one of us shall give account of himself to God".* (Romans 14:12)

2. **Watch.** (v.36-40)
   Be alert and not caught by surprise. Jesus Christ's return will be like a thief, unexpected and unannounced.

   > *"For yourselves know perfectly that the day of the Lord so cometh as a thief in the night."* (1 Thessalonians 5:2)

   > *"But know this, that if the Goodman of the house had known in what watch the thief would come, he would have not suffered his house to be broken up. Therefore, be ye also ready for in such an hour as ye think not the Son of Man cometh."* (Matthew 24:43)

   > *"Behold I come as a thief. Blessed is he that watcheth and keepeth his garments, lest he walk naked and they see his shame."* (Revelation 16:15)

3. **Work.** (vv.41-42). "doing". Some believers are mistaken if they think all they have to do is watch and wait for God.

>*"Moreover it is required in stewards that a man be found faithful."* (1 Corinthians 4:2)

>To be a *"ruler over his household"* (v.42)

4. **Win.** (vv.43-44).

>*"But as it is written, Eye hath not seen, nor ear heard, neither have entered into the heart of man, the things which God hath prepared for them that love him."* (1 Corinthians 2:9)

B. The **Unfaithful Servant.** (vv.45-46)

1. **Careless.** (v.45)
This servant is indifferent to his responsibility to be *"redeeming the time"* (v.48)

>*"Redeeming the time, because the days are evil."* (Ephesians 5:16)

>*"Walk in wisdom toward them that are without, redeeming the time."* (Colossians 4:5)

2. **Cruel.** (v.45)
He thinks only of himself. He has no regard for the well-being of others.

3. **Confident.** (v.46)
He is secure in his behavior. He does not believe that God will judge according to his works.

4. **Confronted.** (vv.46-48)
When the Lord comes, this "servant" will be exposed for what he is; an unbeliever. He is given the *"portion with the unbelievers."* His punishment will be fair and proportional. His sin is willful and open rebellion.

C. **Untrained Servant.**
Other servants who didn't know the Lord's will through indifference or ignorance (immaturity in the faith) will suffer some loss of rewards. teaches that after our salvation, each one of us is building a life, to please God or ourselves. (1 Corinthians 3:11-15)

11 *"For other foundation can no man lay than that is laid, which is Jesus Christ.*
12 *Now if any man build upon this foundation gold, silver, precious stones, wood, hay, stubble;*
13 *every man's work shall be manifest: for the day shall declare it, because it shall be revealed by fire; and the fire shall try every man's work of what sort it is.*
14 *If any man's work abide which he hath build thereupon, he shall receive a reward.*
15 *If any man's work shall be burned, he shall suffer loss: but he himself shall be saved; yet so as by fire."*

What can we learn?

Five thoughts:

1. We all are building.
2. Some of what we build is valuable, some is not.

3. Not everything we do is worthy of reward.
4. God will judge what we do with our live.
5. Be ready for Christ's return.

Make sure your foundation is Jesus Christ.

IV. The Lord's **Judgment.** (vv.47-48)

A. Disobedience brings loss of reward and position.

B. Knowledge brings responsibility and accountability.

V. Some **Observations.**

A. We are either obedient or disobedient.

B. We all shall give an account.

> "*So then every one of us shall give account of himself to God.*" (Romans 14:12)

> "*There is nothing covered, that shall not be revealed; and hid that shall not be known.*" (Matthew 10:26)

Lesson 9-1
Application

1. Are you obedient or disobedient in your Christian walk?

2. Why do many Christians feel little concern about living committed Christian lives?

3. If you could improve one area of your walk with God, what would that be?

4. Are you ready for the Lord's return?

Lesson 9-2

The Parable of the Shrewd and Unjust Steward

Luke 16:1-13

Luke 16:1-13

¹ And he said also unto his disciples, There was a certain rich man, which had a steward; and the same was accused unto him that he had wasted his goods.

² And he called him, and said unto him, How is it that I hear this of thee? give an account of your stewardship; for you may be no longer steward.

³ Then the steward said within himself, What shall I do? for my lord takes away from me the stewardship: I cannot dig; to beg I am ashamed.

⁴ I am resolved what to do, that, when I am put out of the stewardship, they may receive me into their houses.

⁵ So he called every one of his lord's debtors unto him, and said to the first, How much owe you unto my lord?

⁶ And he said, An hundred measures of oil. And he said to him, Take your bill, and sit down quickly, and write fifty.

⁷ Then said he to another, And how much owe you? And he said, An hundred measures of wheat. And he said unto him, Take your bill, and write fourscore.

⁸ And the lord commended the unjust steward, because he had done wisely: for the children of this world are in their generation wiser than the children of light.

⁹ *And I say unto you, Make to yourselves friends by no means the money of unrighteousness, that, when it fails, they may receive you into everlasting habitations.*

¹⁰ *He that is faithful in that which is least is faithful also in much: And he that is unjust in the least is unjust also in much.*

¹¹ *If, therefore, ye have not been faithful in the unrighteous money, who will commit to your trust the true riches?*

¹² *And if you have not been faithful in that which is another man's who shall give your that which is your own?*

¹³ *No servant can serve two masters: For either he will hate the one, and love the other; Or else he will hold to the one, and despise the other. You cannot serve God and money.*

Lesson 9-2

In this parable, the steward is not accused of being dishonest but rather of being a poor manager. Apparently, large debts were owed and were not being collected. Having failed in his present position, this steward prepared for his future. Jesus does not commend dishonesty. (vv.10-12)

I. The **Setting.**

A. Perea is the valley area in which the Jordan river flows.

B. Three months before Christ's death.

C. To his disciples.

II. The **Story.** "A Steward wasted his master's goods."

   A. The Steward.

      1. He built friendship with money.
      2. He used his current position to prepare himself a future position.
      3. He evaluated his options: too weak to do physical labor, and too proud to beg.

> "A prudent man forseeth the evil,
> and hideth himself: but the simple
> pass on, and are punished."
> (Proverbs 22:3)

      4. The Steward called in all the debtors and discounted their debts.

         a. One hundred measures of olive oil is about 850 gallons, which was reduced to only 50 measures of olive oil.
         b. One hundred measure of wheat is roughly 1100 gallons, which was reduced to 80 measures of wheat, or 275 gallons.

   B. The **Rich Man.**

      1. Discovered the treachery.
      2. Commended the Steward.

   What is surprising is the response. This rich man must have been very rich indeed.

III. Some Observations.

   A. Money if used wisely can accomplish great things for God.

   B. Be prepared for the future.

Lesson 9-2
The Application

1. Why do you think some people are prepared for eternity, and some are not?

2. How can we use our resources to further the kingdom of God?

3. What did the unjust steward do right?

   Do wrong?

4. What would you do if you were in a similar situation?

Lesson 9-3

Parable of the Rich Man and Lazarus

Luke 16:19-31

Luke 16:19-31

¹⁹ *There was a certain rich man, which was clothed in purple and fine linen, and fared sumptuously every day:*

²⁰ *And there was a certain beggar named Lazarus, which was laid at his gate, full of sores,*

²¹ *And desiring to be fed with the crumbs which fell from the rich man's table: moreover the dogs came and licked his sores.*

²² *And it came to pass, that the beggar died, and was carried by the angels into Abraham's bosom: the rich man also died, and was buried;*

²³ *And in hell he lifted up his eyes, being in torments, and saw Abraham afar off, and Lazarus in his bosom.*

²⁴ *And he cried and said, Father Abraham, have mercy on me, and send Lazarus, that he may dip the tip of his finger in water, and cool my tongue; for I am tormented in this flame.*

²⁵ *But Abraham said, Son, remember that thou in thy lifetime received thy good things, and likewise Lazarus evil things: but now he is comforted, and thou art tormented.*

²⁶ *And beside all this, between us and you there is a great gulf fixed: so that they which would pass from*

hence to you cannot; neither can they pass to us, that would come from thence.

27 Then he said, I pray you therefore, father, that thou would send him to my father's house:

28 For I have five brethren; that he may testify unto them, lest they also come into this place of torment.

29 Abraham saith unto him, They have Moses and the prophets; let them hear them.

30 And he said, Nay, father Abraham: but if one went unto them from the dead, they will repent.

31 And he said unto him, If they hear not Moses and the prophets, neither will they be persuaded, though one rose from the dead.

Lesson 9-3

I. The **Setting.**

    A. Set between two parables, The Unjust Steward, (Luke 16:1-13) [see Lesson 9-2], and Unprofitable Servant, (Luke 17:6-10) [see Lesson 7-1]. This after reproving the Pharisees for covetousness, (v.14) and after teaching about self-righteousness and divorce. (v13–16)

    B. Some people make a mockery of hell. Many, including the cults, deny the reality of hell or think they are too good to go there. Jesus spoke often about hell because there is a future judgment that will fall upon each unsaved person.

II. The **Uniqueness** of this Story.

    A. The use of personal names is unique, and only used in this story:

        1. Abraham six times.

(vss. 22, 23, 24, 25, 29, 30)

   2. Lazarus four times. (vss. 20, 23, 24, 25)

   3. Moses two times. (vss. 29, 31)
     If this is a parable, what do these names represent?

B. The problem of consistency with other parables?

   1. What is the underlying reality? In other words, what reality would Jesus hearers identify with and relate to a new spiritual truth?

   2. If death is merely the grave, what is the point of this "parable"?

C. Parables are always established on reality.
There is a literal reality that is used to explain a spiritual truth. The listeners could see this reality in their mind because it was part of everyday life.

D. If you really believe the Bible, you must believe in **heaven, and hell**. If death is merely a grave, what is the point of this story?

III. The **Reality** of Hell.
The Jewish leaders of Jesus' day thought that because they were Abraham's descendants, they would be saved from future judgment, relying on Abraham's covenant with God. (Genesis 12:1-3)

> [7] "But when he saw many of the Pharisees and Sadducees come to his baptism, he said unto them, Oh generation of vipers, who hath warned you to flee from the wrath to come?
> [8] Bring forth therefore fruits meet for repentance.
> [9] And think not to say within yourselves, We have Abraham to our father: for I say unto you,

that God is able of these stones to raise up children unto Abraham.

10 And now also the axe is laid unto the root of the trees, therefore, every tree which bringeth not forth good fruit, is hewn down, and cast into the fire.

11 I indeed baptize you with water unto repentance. But He that cometh after me is mightier than I, whose shoes I am not worthy to bear: he shall baptize you with the Holy Ghost, and with fire.

12 Whose fan is in His hand, and He will thoroughly purge His floor, and gather His wheat into the garner, but He will burn up the chaff with unquenchable fire."

(Matthew 3:7-12)

The Lord Jesus spoke often about the future judgment that would fall on each person who rejected him as the Messiah. So terrible is the concept of hell that Jesus warned to flee from the future judgment:

27 "Ye have heard that it was said by them of old time, Thou shalt not commit adultery.

28 But I say unto you, That whosoever looketh on a woman to lust after her hath committed adultery with her already in his heart.

29 And if thy right eye offends thee, pluck it out, and cast it from thee: for it is profitable for thee that one of thy members should perish, and not that thy whole body should be cast into hell.

30 And if thy right hand offend thee, cut it off, and cast it from thee: for it is profitable for thee that one of thy members should perish, and not that thy whole body should be cast into hell." (Matthew 5:27-30)

43 "And if thy hand offend thee, cut it off: it is better for thee to enter into life maimed than having two hands to go into hell, into the fire that never shall be quenched:

44 Where their worm dieth not, and the fire is not quenched.

45 And if thy foot offend thee, cut it off, it is better for thee to enter halt into life, than having two feet to be cast into hell, unto the fire that never shall be quenched:

46 Where their worm dieth not, and the fire is not quenched:

47 And if thine eye offend thee, pluck it out: it is better for thee to enter into the kingdom of God with one eye, than having two eyes to be cast into hell fire:

48 Where their worm dieth not, and the fire is not quenched." (Mark 9:43-48)

IV. What did the rich man **experience** in Hell?

   A. He could **see.** (v.23) He could see where he was.

      1. Flame.
      2. People. Abraham and Lazarus.
      3. Comfort.
      4. Fixed Gulf.

   B. He Could **Remember.** (vv.23,25)

      1. His former life.
      2. Abraham, though we don't know if he had ever met him.
      3. Lazarus.
      4. His brothers.

C. He could **speak.** (vv.24-30) Note what he said.

  1. Have **mercy.** (v.24) He never once questioned why he was in hell.
  2. I am **tormented.** (v.24.) The flames in hell are real.
  3. I **pray** thee. (vv.27-28) Prayers are not answered in hell. "*Warn my brothers and father's house.*" He never wants to see his family with him again.
  4. Send him to my father's house. (v.27)
  5. Testify unto them. (v.28)
  6. They will repent. (v.30)
  7. He did not say:
      a. How great he was.
      b. Complain about hell being unfair.

D. He could **hear.** (v.25) He carried on a conversation with Abraham.

E. He could **Feel.** (vv.23-24)

  1. Being in torment by this flame. (v.23)
  2. Cool my tongue. (v.24)
  3. In this flame. (v.24) How can something burn and not be consumed. Consider Moses and the burning bush. (Exodus 31)

V. The Rich Man's **Request**. (vv.24-28)

  A. Mercy, unmerited forgiveness. (v.24)

  B. Send Lazarus with water. (v.24)

  C. Send Lazarus to my brethren. (vv.27-28)

VI. Abraham's **Response.** (vv.29-31)

A. There is a great gulf fixed, (bottomless pit?).

> "And I saw an angel come down
> from heaven, having the key of the
> bottomless pit and a great chain in
> his hand." (Revelation 20:1)

B. Lazarus cannot come to you or your brethren. (v.31)

C. If your brethren will not hear Moses and the prophets, neither will they be persuaded though one rose from the dead. (v.31) Miracles do not confirm truth to an unbeliever. Man believes what he chooses to believe.

VII. The **Reason.** The rich man was in hell. (v.30) He failed to repent. Therefore, all that remains is judgment. How will God judge?

A. **Words.**

> "But I say unto you, That every idle
> word that men shall speak, they shall
> give account thereof in the day of
> judgment." (Matthew 12:36)

B. **Deeds.**

> "For there is nothing covered, that
> shall not be revealed; neither hid,
> that shall not be known. Also I say
> unto you, Whosoever shall confess
> me before men, him shall the Son of
> man also confess before the angels
> of God: But he that denieth me

before men shall be denied before the angels of God."
(Luke 12:2, 8-9)

C. **Belief.**

"He that believeth on him is not condemned: but he that believeth not is condemned already, because he hath not believed in the name of the only begotten Son of God." (John 3:18)

VIII. The **Hopelessness** of Hell. (v.26)

The saddest thing about hell is there is no way out. Forever, this man is cut off from God. There is no comfort or relief. God's love is not present. There is no mercy, only a loneliness and time to remember for all eternity.

Some Observations:

A. Hell is permanent.

B. No complaint about his punishment being unfair.

C. Miracles do not produce faith.

Lesson 9-3
Application

1. Is this a parable or not?

   Why?

2. What does this story teach?

3. What difference should this story make in our lives?

4. What do you plan to do to reach your lost loved ones?

5. When do you plan to witness to them?

LESSON 9-4

THE PARABLE OF THE ABSENT HOUSEHOLDER

MASTER'S RETURN

Mark 13:34-37

Mark 13:34-37

³⁴ For the Son of man is as a man taking a far journey, who left his house, and gave authority to his servants, and to every man his work, and commanded the porter to watch.
³⁵ Watch ye therefore: for ye know not when the master of the house comes, at evening, or at midnight, or at the cockcrowing, or in the morning:
³⁶ Lest coming suddenly he find you sleeping.
³⁷ And what I say unto you I say unto all, Watch.

Lesson 9-4

I. The **Setting.**

A. After viewing the temple with his disciples and foretelling its destruction. (v.1)

B. As Jesus sat upon the Mount of Olives. (v.3)

C. After warning about the tribulation. (vv.21-24)

II. The **Story.** "a man taking a far journey."

A. The Man is Christ.

B. Servants and Porter are believers.

> *"Moreover it is required in stewards, that a man be found faithful."* (1 Corinthians 4:2)

C. Lord's Return. Christ's second coming.

III. The **Command.** Watch.
We see an allusion to the Roman watch which was three hours in length. A Roman watch began at 9:00 PM. corresponding with the "even" was changed at 12:00 PM. corresponding with "midnight", again at 3:00 AM corresponding with "cockcrowing" and finally at 6:00 AM. corresponding with "morning".

A. We are to be diligent. *"while men slept."* (Parable of the tares, Matthew 13:25)
Doctrinal error has entered into the church because people were too indifferent to deal with the error.

B. We need to be serving.

> *"All scripture is given by inspiration of God, and is profitable for doctrine, for reproof, for correction, for instruction in righteousness: That the man of God may be perfect, thoroughly furnished unto all good works."*
> (2 Timothy 3:16-17)

As we come to the end of the age, it will be more pressing to watch and serve.

Lesson 9-4
Application

1. How can you prepare yourself to identify danger?

2. What is the greatest threat to believers in this day and age?

3. What should you be doing to resist this danger?

4. Why are some Christians "asleep"?

5. What are you personally doing to watch and serve?

LESSON 9-5

PARABLE OF THE WEDDING GARMENT

INVITATION TO A WEDDING

Matthew 22:1-14

Matthew 22:1-14

1 And Jesus answered and spoke to them again by parables, and said,

2 The kingdom of heaven is like to a certain king, which made a marriage for his son,

3 And sent forth his servants to call them that were bidden to the wedding: and they would not come.

4 Again, he sent forth other servants, saying, Tell them which are bidden, Behold, I have prepared my dinner: my oxen and my fatlings are killed, and all things are ready: come to the marriage.

5 But they made light of it, and went their ways, one to his farm, another to his merchandise:

6 And the remnant took his servants, and entreated them spitefully, and slew them.

7 But when the king heard thereof, he was wroth: and he sent forth his armies, and destroyed those murderers, and burned up their city.

8 Then saith he to his servants, the wedding is ready, but they which were bidden were not worthy.

9 Go ye therefore into the highways, and as many as you shall find, bid to the marriage.

10 *So those servants went out into the highways, and gathered together all as many as they found, both bad and good: and the wedding was furnished with guests.*

11 *And when the king came in to see the guests, he saw there a man which had not on a wedding garment:*

12 *And he saith unto him, Friend, how came thou in here not having a wedding garment? And he was speechless.*

13 *Then said the king to the servants, Bind him hand and foot, and take him away, and cast him into outer darkness; there shall be weeping and gnashing of teeth.*

14 *For many are called, but few are chosen.*

Lesson 9-5

This parable, is similar to the Wedding Feast, recorded in Luke 12:35-48, yet there are some important differences. This parable was uttered in the temple at Jerusalem. while the parable of the wedding feast was spoken at the house of a Pharisee where Jesus was invited to enjoy a meal.

In Luke's parable of the wedding feast, the guests were discourteous. They are merely shut out of the wedding feast. In Matthew's parable of the wedding garment, they are destroyed and their city is burned. The element of the wedding garment is unique to this parable and has no parallel in the wedding feast.

As in other parables, the king represents God the Father, and the son is Jesus Christ. The servants are the prophets who are faithfully serving God. Those "bidden" to the feast are the Jews. This parable was spoken a few days before Christ's arrest and crucifixion.

I. The **Invitation.** (vv.3-4)

    A. God gives an invitation to all to come to salvation.

> *"For God so loved the world, that he gave his only begotten Son, that whosoever believeth in him should not perish, but have everlasting life."* (John 3:16)

    B. God gives an invitation to salvation but never an edict.

> *"All that the Father giveth me shall come to me; and him that cometh to me I will in no wise cast out."* (John 6:37)

    C. God provides all that is necessary for salvation.

> *"For by grace are ye saved through faith; and that not of yourselves; it is the gift of God; Not of works, lest any man should boast."* (Ephesians 2:8-9)

II. The **Rejection.**
The Jews of Jesus' day committed four grave sins. (vv.5-8)

    A. They **made light** of it. (v.5)

    B. They **mistreated** the king's servants. (v.6)

    C. They **killed** those who invited them. (v.6)

    D. They brought **judgment** on themselves. (v.7)

The anger of the king resulted in the sending forth of his armies to destroy them and burn up the city. His evaluation was: *"they which were bidden not worthy."* (v.8) Jerusalem was destroyed in 70 A.D. by the Roman General Titus. The temple was destroyed and burned with fire. It is estimated that more than one million people perished through hunger, disease and the sword. Countless numbers of people were crucified by the Romans when captured in battle.

III. The **Substitution.**

Having a feast and not guests, the king orders his servants to invite others.

This could be anyone, including Gentiles.

A. The servants **gathered** everyone they could. (vv.9-10)

B. Some guests were "**good**", and others "**bad**". (v.10)

    The "good" and "bad" in this parable do not refer to salvation, they refer to their appearance and reputation. Only God can tell who is, and who is not saved.

C. All guests were given a **wedding garment.** (vv.11-12)

    It was a custom in some parts of the Middle East to supply royal guests with a simple robe to signify acceptance to the wedding supper and provided a uniformity of appearance.

D. One guest **ignored** wearing the king's wedding garment. (v.12)

    He refused to come to the king's table on the king's terms. The "wedding garment" represents salvation. For a guest entering without a wedding garment would be a grave insult. This guest willingly chose to ignore what was provided. The end result was his judgment and eternal loss. The guest's speechlessness conforms well to Romans 3:19, "*...that every mouth may be stopped, and all the world may become guilty before God.*" This guest was disobedient and presumptuous.

> "*But we are all as an unclean thing, and all our righteousness are as filthy rags; and we all do fade as a leaf; and our iniquities, like the wind, have taken us away.*"
> (Isaiah 64:6)

E. We must come to God on **His terms** or suffer the consequences.
We are absolutely unworthy of salvation. The best works we have are unable to secure our salvation and a place at the table in heaven. God will not lower His standard of salvation. (vv.13-14)

F. The **speechless** guest. (vv.12-13)
Instead of enjoying the feast, he is removed. Self-righteousness is no righteousness at all. The "outer darkness" and "weeping and gnashing of teeth" is a common phrase used of judgment in hell.

Lesson 9-5
Application

1. How many ways are there to salvation?

   Acts 4:12

2. Why is it important to receive God's way of salvation?

3. What happens to those who make light of God's way of salvation?

4. Have you received God's way of salvation?

5. Would any of your friends rather go to hell, to be with their friends, instead of going to heaven?

   Is this reasonable?

LESSON 9-6

THE PARABLE OF THE TEN VIRGINS

Matthew 25:1-13

Matthew 25:1-13

1 Then shall the kingdom of heaven be like to ten virgins, which took their lamps, and went forth to meet the bridegroom.

2 And five of them were wise, and five were foolish.

3 They that were foolish took their lamps, and took no oil with them:

4 But the wise took oil in their vessels with their lamps.

5 While the bridegroom tarried, they all slumbered and slept.

6 And at midnight there was a cry made, Behold, the bridegroom cometh; go you out to meet him.

7 Then all those virgins arose, and trimmed their lamps.

8 And the foolish said to the wise, Give us of your oil; for our lamps are gone out.

9 But the wise answered, saying, Not so; lest there be not enough for us and you: but go you rather to them that sell, and buy for yourselves.

10 And while they went to buy, the bridegroom came; and they that were ready went in with him to the marriage: and the door was shut.

11 Afterward came also the other virgins, saying, Lord, Lord, open to us.

12 But he answered and said, Verily I say unto you, I know you not.

13 Watch therefore, for ye know neither the day nor the hour wherein the Son of man cometh.

Lesson 9-6

I. The **Setting.**

After teaching about His Second Coming, Jesus warns about being ready when he returns. This parable speaks of the continuation of the kingdom of heaven.

II. The **Story.**

All ten virgins were bridesmaids who attended to the bride prior to her marriage. They took their lamps and went forth to keep the bride company until the bridegroom arrived. It was the custom in Jesus' day for the bridegroom to arrive unannounced at night to take his bride away. So the bride and her attendants needed to be ready at a moment's notice of his arrival. The bridegroom would then bring the bride back to his own home for the wedding ceremony and feast.

Notice the bridesmaids.

A. How they were all the same.

1. Each was dressed in the same garments of a **bridesmaids**.
2. Each **acted** like the others.
3. Each had the **same purpose**.
4. Each was a virgin – **professing believers**.
5. All expected to meet the bridegroom.
6. All had some oil.

B. How they were different.

1. Half of them **were wise** and prepared.
2. The other half **were foolish** and unprepared.

III. The **Shortage.** (vv.2-4)

    A. While these bridesmaids looked and acted alike, there was one very important difference. They all had some oil in their lamps, the wise had full lamps, but the foolish only had enough oil for the moment. When it was time for the bridegroom to come and take away his bride, only the wise had enough oil to continue with the bride. The foolish had no more oil. Lamps without oil are useless!

    B. Imagery.

        1. Virgins. Professing believers.
        2. Bridegroom. Christ.
        3. Oil. Holy Spirit.

    C. For example: Oil in the Bible is often used as a symbol of the Holy Spirit.

> *"The Spirit of the Lord is upon me, because he hath anointed me to preach the gospel."* (Luke 4:18)

Five foolish bridesmaids were without oil or the Holy Spirit.

> *"Now if any man have not the Spirit of Christ, he is none of his."* (Romans 8:9)

IV. The **Shame.**

    A. Consider:

        1. All had some oil. This suggests that they all had some exposure to the truth. The wise took in the truth which resulted in salvation,

and; the foolish took only enough to appear religious.

2. What faith each of us has is sufficient only for ourselves. The foolish seek to buy oil from others, but cannot.
3. Our salvation is personal.
4. Failure to be ready results in rejection.

B. There must be a lot of unsaved people in the visible church today.

> "But be ye doers of the word, and not hearers only, deceiving your own selves." (James 1:22)

C. The Warning.

> "Watch therefore for ye know neither the day nor the hour wherein the Son of man cometh." (Matthew 25:13)

V. The **Sleep.** (vv.5-6)
The sleep of the wise and foolish certainly pictures the church in our present age.

> "Watch therefore; for ye know not what hour your Lord doth come, therefore, be ye also ready for in such an hour as ye think not the Son of Man cometh." (Matthew 24:42,44)

> "For yourselves know perfectly that the day of the Lord so cometh as a thief in the night." (1 Thessalonians 5:2)

VI. The **Surprise.** v.7-9
The foolish maidens passed for a while but their lamps would not stay lit. They did not possess what

they needed (salvation) and they tried to borrow from the wise bridesmaids. Salvation, however, cannot be borrowed. The foolish bridesmaids came up short.

VII. The **Separation.** (vv.10-12)
The door to the feast was shut and the foolish were caught outside. Like Noah, when God shut the door to the ark, no one could come in. It was closed for good. They were unprepared. The wise will inherit eternal life with Jesus. The foolish, will receive eternal judgment and separation from God.

VIII. The **Solution.** (v.13)

A. **Watch.**
Jesus is coming. (Matthew 24:42)

B. **Be Ready.**
Jesus offers salvation. (Matthew 24:44)

Lesson 9-6
Application

1. Why do you think the wise were ready for the bridegroom's coming?

2. Why were the foolish not prepared?

3. What have you done to be prepared for Christ's coming?

4. How do you know you are saved and on your way to heaven?

LESSON 9-7

THE PARABLE OF THE
SHEEP AND GOATS

Matthew 25:31-46

Matthew 25:31-46

31 When the Son of man shall come in his glory, and all the holy angels with him, then shall he sit upon the throne of his glory:

32 And before him shall be gathered all nations: and he shall separate them one from another, as a shepherd divides his sheep from the goats:

33 And he shall set the sheep on his right hand, but the goats on the left.

34 Then shall the King say unto them on his right hand, Come, you blessed of my Father, inherit the kingdom prepared for you from the foundation of the world:

35 For I was an hungry, and you gave me meat: I was thirsty, and you gave me drink: I was a stranger, and you took me in:

36 Naked, and you clothed me: I was sick, and you visited me: I was in prison, and you came unto me.

37 Then shall the righteous answer him, saying, Lord, when we saw you were hungry, and fed you? or thirsty, and gave you drink?

38 When saw we you a stranger, and took you in? or naked, and clothed you?

39 Or when saw we you sick, or in prison, and came to you?

⁴⁰ *And the King shall answer and say to them, Verily I say to you, Inasmuch as you have done it to one of the least of these my brethren, you have done it to me.*

⁴¹ *Then shall he say also to them on the left hand, Depart from me, you cursed, into everlasting fire, prepared for the devil and his angels:*

⁴² *For I was an hungry, and you gave me no meat: I was thirsty, and ye gave me no drink:*

⁴³ *I was a stranger, and you took me not in: naked, and you clothed me not: sick, and in prison, and you visited me not.*

⁴⁴ *Then shall they also answer him, saying, Lord, when we saw you as hungry, or thirsty, or a stranger, or naked, or sick, or in prison, and did not minister to you?*

⁴⁵ *Then shall he answer them, saying, Verily I say to you, Inasmuch as you did it not to one of the least of these, you did it not to me.*

⁴⁶ *And these shall go away into everlasting punishment: but the righteous into life eternal.*

Lesson 9-7

What will happen when Christ returns to establish his kingdom on earth? This parable answers some of the questions concerning future judgment.

I. The **Setting.**

    A. Given on the Mount of Olives. (Matthew 24:3)
       The Mount of Olives is a small range of four summits that overlook Jerusalem and the Temple Mount across the Kidron Valley (Garden of Gethsemane) from the east. It is 2,723 feet high. The Mount of

Olives is more than a mile in length and composed of limestone. It runs north and south though it bends west to enclose the city on three sides.

B. Given in response to his disciples' questions concerning the end of the world. (Matthew 24:3)

C. Part of the Mount of Olives discourse. (Matthew 24-25)

II. The **Story.** "When the Son of Man shall come in His glory."

A. Shepherd. Jesus Christ.

B. Sheep. Saved.

> "I am the good shepherd, and know my sheep, and am known of mine." (John 10:14)

C. Goats. Lost.

D. "And Aaron shall bring the goat upon which the Lord's lot fell, and offer him for a sin offering." (Leviticus 16:9)

III. Where will these **people** be judged?

A. On earth, not heaven.

B. Near the Mount of Olives.

> "And his feet shall stand in that day upon the Mount of Olives, which is before Jerusalem on the east, and the Mount of Olives shall cleave in the midst thereof toward the east and toward the west, and there shall be a very great valley; and half of

the mountain shall remove toward the north, and half of it toward the south." (Zechariah 14:4)

C. In the Valley of Jehoshaphat – (literally *"Jehovah will Judge"*) probably in this valley created by the Lord's return.

"*I will also gather all nations, and will bring them down into the Valley of Jehoshaphat, and will plead with them there for my people and for my heritage Israel, whom they have scattered among the nations and parted my land."*
(Joel 3:2)

IV. The **Judgment** of the Nations.

A. The Saved. Right hand (sheep).

1. Their Works.

    "*Wherefore by their fruits ye shall know them."* (Matthew 7:20)

2. Their Reward. Life eternal.

B. The Lost. Left hand (goats).

1. Their Works.
2. Their Reward. Everlasting fire.

V. Some Observations:

A. God had a plan from the very beginning (v.34): eternal life for the saved, judgment for the lost.

B. God looks on our service to others as service to him. (v.40)

Lesson 9-7
Application

1. Are you a sheep, or a goat?

2. How do you know?

3. What works did the righteous do?

4. What did Jesus say concerning those who do good works?

5. What works of righteousness are you doing?

INDEX

PARABLE LESSONS

The parables of Jesus Christ, covered in this book, had different titles, depending on which edition, age, or translation of the Bible being used. Below are many of those different titles, and links to the parable lessons used in our study.

Absent Householder	9-4
Barren Fig Tree	8-3
Drag Net	2-8
Fig Tree	8-7
Foolish and Wise Builders	6-1
Friend at Midnight	4-1
Good Samaritan	6-2
Good Shepherd	6-3
Great Supper	8-4
Growing Seed	2-3
Hidden Treasure	2-6
Hours	7-3
Householder	2-9
House on the Rock	6-1
In the Field	2-6
Invitation to a Wedding Feast	9-5

Leaven	2-5
Lost Coin	3-3
Lost Sheep	3-2
Lost Son	3-4
Marriage of King's Son	9-5
Master's Return	9-4
Master and Servant	7-1
Minas and Pounds	7-2
Moneylender Forgives Debts	5-2
Mustard Seed	2-4
New Cloth	8-1
New Wine	8-2
Obedient Servant	7-1
Owner of a House	2-9
Pearl of Great Price	2-7
Persistent Widow and Unjust Judge	4-2
Pharisee and Publican	4-3
Prodigal Son	3-4
Rich Fool	3-1
Rich Man and Lazarus	9-3
Sheep and Goats	9-7
Shrewd and Unjust Steward	9-2
Sower	2-1
Talents	7-4
Ten Pounds (Minas)	7-2
Ten Virgins	9-6
Two Debtors	5-2
Two Foundations	6-1
Two Sons	8-5
Unjust Judge	4-2
Unjust Steward	9-2

Unmerciful Servant   5-1

Unprofitable Servant   7-1

Valuable Pearl   2-7

Vineyard Laborers   7-3

Virgins   9-6

Watchful and Foolish Servants   9-1

Wedding Garment   9-5

Weeds   2-2

Wheat and Tares   2-2

Wicked Tenants   8-6

Workers in the Vineyard   7-3

ABOUT THE AUTHORS

ART ZACHER

Art Zacher was pastor of Berean Baptist Church in Fairfield, California from 1999 to 2022. His interest in seeing others come to Christ led him to help others start churches in Connecticut and New York. After graduating from seminary, he started Victory Baptist Church in Thomaston, Connecticut. He has been a teacher and principal in various Christian schools.

Brother Art graduated from Illinois State University in 1978 with a B.S. in Business Administration, and a minor in Speech Communication. He received his Master of Divinity from Temple Baptist Theological Seminary in Chattanooga, Tennessee in 1982.

Pastor Zacher, with his wife Melodie, have been socially active in their community, meeting the physical, spiritual, and emotional needs through outreach. In January 2022, they moved to Greenville, SC, to be with their grandchildren. They have three grown daughters and eight grandchildren.

He can be contacted at artzacher@sbcglobal.net, and is available for speaking engagements.

Doug Peterson

Doug Peterson is a retired Coast Guard officer and combat veteran, who served for 27 years. While in the military, he led many Bible study groups and classes, at various military commands where there was no chaplain.

Brother Doug graduated with honors from Chaminade University of Honolulu in 1985. After his retirement, he served at the California Maritime Academy as their historical archivist, helping to preserve the history and documents of that school.

Mr. Peterson is an ordained Baptist Deacon, minister, and Bible teacher. He has served in many churches, being involved in various duties and responsibilities. Doug Peterson and Art Zacher worked together for many years at Art's church, as a teacher and assistant to the Pastor, and now on this book.

Doug and his wife Roberta are now retired in Kentucky, with three successful sons and their families, including fourteen grandchildren.

Photo by Melodie Zacher © 2021

Art Zacher   and   Doug Peterson

"AMEN !"   "GOD BLESS YOU."
I Corinthians 4:2   *Philippians 4:4*

POST TENEBRAS LUX

Martin Luther

"After darkness, Light"

Printed in the United States
by Baker & Taylor Publisher Services